Bountiful Earth

Pam Schiller

Special Needs Adaptations by Clarissa Willis

Acknowledgments

I would like to thank the following people for their contributions to this book. The special needs adaptations were written by Clarissa Willis. The CD is arranged by Patrick

Clarissa Willis   Patrick Brennan   Richele Bartkowiak

Brennan, and performed by Richele Bartkowiak and Patrick Brennan. It was engineered and mixed by Jeff Smith at Southwest Recordings. —Pam Schiller

Books written by Pam Schiller

The Bilingual Book of Rhymes, Songs, Stories, and Fingerplays, with Rafael Lara-Alecio and Beverly J. Irby

The Complete Book of Activities, Games, Stories, Props, Recipes, and Dances, with Jackie Silberg

The Complete Book of Rhymes, Songs, Poems, Fingerplays, and Chants, with Jackie Silberg

The Complete Daily Curriculum for Early Childhood: Over 1200 Easy Activities to Support Multiple Intelligences and Learning Styles, with Pat Phipps

The Complete Resource Book: An Early Childhood Curriculum, with Kay Hastings

The Complete Resource Book for Infants: Over 700 Experiences for Children From Birth to 18 Months

The Complete Resource Book for Toddlers and Twos: Over 2000 Experiences and Ideas

Count on Math: Activities for Small Hands and Lively Minds, with Lynne Peterson

Creating Readers: Over 1000 Games, Activities, Tongue Twisters, Fingerplays, Songs, and Stories to Get Children Excited About Reading

Do You Know the Muffin Man?, with Thomas Moore

The Instant Curriculum, Revised, with Joan Rosanno

The Practical Guide to Quality Child Care, with Patricia Carter Dyke

Start Smart: Building Brain Power in the Early Years

The Values Book, with Tamera Bryant

Where Is Thumbkin?, with Thomas Moore

Bountiful Earth

CD INSIDE!

25 Songs and Over 300 Activities for Young Children

Pam Schiller

Gryphon House, Inc.
Beltsville, Maryland

Bountiful Earth

© 2006 Pam Schiller
Printed in the United States of America.

Illustrations: Deborah Johnson
Cover Art: Photogaph by Richele Bartkowiak, ©2005.

Published by Gryphon House, Inc.
10726 Tucker Street, Beltsville, MD 20705
301.595.9500; 301.595.0051 (fax); 800.638.0928 (toll-free)

Visit us on the web at www.ghbooks.com

 Gryphon House is a member of the Green Press Initiative, a nonprofit program dedicated to supporting publishers in their efforts to reduce their use of fiber sourced forests. For further information visit www.greenpressinitiative.org

Library of Congress Cataloging-in-Publication Data
Schiller, Pamela Byrne.
  Bountiful earth / Pam Schiller and Richele Bartkowiak ; special needs adaptations by Clarissa Willis.
       p. cm.
  Includes bibliographical references (p.   ) and index.
  ISBN-13: 978-0-87659-016-4 (alk. paper)
  ISBN-10: 0-87659-016-4 (alk. paper)
 1. Music--Instruction and study--Juvenile. 2. Early childhood education. 3. Education, Preschool. 4. Children's songs. I. Bartkowiak, Richele. II. Willis, Clarissa. III. Title.
  MT920.S37 2006
  372.87'044--dc22

                                        2005034968

Table of Contents

Introduction

Music in the Early Years

Music is a universal language, and singing is a hallmark of the early childhood classroom. Children love to sing! Teachers love to sing! Age makes no difference. Culture makes no difference.

Singing songs enriches thematic content, supports literacy concepts, and optimizes memory and learning. When you extend classroom activities, including modifications for special needs and English language learner populations, it is a perfect package. *Bountiful Earth* is one of eight thematic book/CD sets that offer all of these resources in one package.

Thematic Content

Bountiful Earth overlaps several typical early childhood themes: Seasons, Weather, The Environment, Growing Things, Nature, and Patriotism. Read the lyrics and decide the best fit in your curriculum for each song.

Every song is accompanied by a list of facts titled "Did You Know?" which offers background information about the song, interesting facts about the topic or lyrics, historical information, or some form of trivia you can use as a springboard to discussion. This will save you hours of research and add significantly to the value of the song.

Literacy Concepts

Young children need experiences that allow them to develop and practice basic literacy skills, such as listening, oral language development, phonological awareness, letter knowledge, print awareness, and comprehension. Suggestions for using the songs in *Bountiful Earth* as a springboard for teaching these literacy skills accompany every title. Below is a definition of each literacy skill and the sub-skills they encompass.

❍ **Listening:** the development of age-appropriate attention span, as well as the ability to listen for a variety of purposes; for example, details, directions, and sounds.

❍ **Oral Language Development:** the acquisition of vocabulary, the fine-tuning of grammar, and the increase in sentence length and complexity.

O **Phonological Awareness:** sensitivity to the sounds of language. Phonological awareness begins with babbling and cooing and goes all the way through the understanding of sound and symbol relationships and decoding. The skills in the higher end of the phonological awareness continuum--sound and symbol relationship and decoding—are appropriate for children who are age five or older.

O **Segmentation:** the breaking apart of words by syllable or letter; for example, children clap the breaks in the word *di-no-saur*.

O **Rhyme:** words that sound alike. The ending sound of the words is the same, but the initial consonant sound is different, for example, *cat* and *hat* or *rake* and *cake*.

O **Alliteration:** the repetition of a consonant sound in a series of words; for example, Peter Piper picked a peck of pickled peppers. Children need to be able to hear the repetition of the /p/ sound, but do not need to identify that the sound is made by the letter "p".

O **Onomatopoeia:** words whose sound suggests the sound they are describing; for example, *pitter-patter, moo, quack, beep,* and so on.

O **Letter Knowledge:** the visual recognition of each letter of the alphabet, both lowercase and uppercase.

O **Print Awareness:** the understanding that print has many functions; for example, telling a story, making a list, as part of signs, in news articles, in recipes, and so on. It is also the awareness that print moves left to right and top to bottom.

O **Comprehension:** the internalization of a story or a concept.

Optimizing Memory and Learning

Singing boosts memory and keeps the brain alert. Increased memory and alertness optimize the potential for learning. When we sing we generally feel good. That sense of well-being causes the brain to release endorphins into the blood stream and those endorphins act as a memory fixative. When we sing we automatically increase our oxygen intake, which, in turn, increases our alertness. Scientific research has validated what early childhood professionals know intuitively—that singing has a positive effect on learning.

Expanding the Children's Learning With Activities

Using songs as a springboard for activities is a good way to bring the lyrics of the song into a meaningful context for children. Exploring different types of clothing after singing a song about winter clothes reinforces and creates a meaningful context for the specific characteristics of winter clothing. Sorting seeds, rolling seeds, eating seeds, and planting seeds after singing "The Seeds Grow" help children better understand the characteristics and use of seeds.

Reading a book about seeds after singing about seeds also helps expand children's understanding. Literature selections are provided for each song. Integrating the teaching of themes and skills with songs, literature, and multidisciplinary activities provides a comprehensive approach for helping children recognize the patterns and the interconnected relationships of what they are learning.

Throughout the book, questions to ask children appear in italics. These questions are intended to help children think and reflect on what they have learned. This reflective process optimizes the opportunity for children to apply the information and experiences they have encountered.

Modifications

Suggestions for children with special needs and suggestions for English language learners accompany the song activities when appropriate. These features allow teachers to use the activities with diverse populations. All children love to sing and the benefits apply to all!

Special Needs

The inclusion of children with disabilities in preschool and child care programs is increasingly common. Parents, teachers, and researchers have found that children benefit in many ways from integrated programs that are designed to meet the needs of all children. Many children with disabilities, however, need accommodations to participate successfully in the general classroom.

Included in the extensions and activities for each song are adaptations for children with special needs. These adaptations allow *all* children to experience the song and related activities in a way that will maximize their learning opportunities. The adaptations are specifically for children who have needs in the following areas:

- sensory integration
- distractibility
- hearing loss
- spatial organization
- language, receptive and expressive
- fine motor coordination
- cognitive challenges

The following general strategies from Kathleen Bulloch (2003) are for children who have difficulty listening and speaking.

Difficulty	Adaptations/Modifications/Strategies
Listening	- State the objective—provide a reason for listening - Use a photo card - Give explanations in small, discrete steps - Be concise with verbal information: "Evan, please sit," instead of "Evan, would you please sit down in your chair?" - Provide visuals - Have the child repeat directions - Have the child close his eyes and try to visualize the information - Provide manipulative tasks - When giving directions to the class, leave a pause between each step so the child can carry out the process in her mind - Shorten the listening time required - Pre-teach difficult vocabulary and concepts
Verbal Expression	- Provide a prompt, such as beginning the sentence for the child or giving a picture cue - Accept an alternate form of information-sharing, such as artistic creation, photos, charade or pantomime, and demonstration - Ask questions that require short answers - Specifically teaching body and language expression - First ask questions at the information level—giving facts and asking for facts back - Wait for children to respond; don't call on the first child to raise his hand - Have the child break in gradually by speaking in smaller groups and then in larger groups

English Language Learners

Strategies for English language learners are also provided to maximize the learning potential for English language learners.

The following are general strategies for working with English language learners (Gray, Fleischman, 2004-05):

○ **Keep the language simple.** Speak simply and clearly. Use short, complete sentences in a normal tone of voice. Avoid using slang, idioms, or figures of speech.

○ **Use actions and illustrations to reinforce oral statements.** Appropriate prompts and facial expressions help convey meaning.

○ **Ask for completion, not generation.** Ask children to choose answers from a list or to complete a partially finished sentence. Encourage children to use language as much as possible to gain confidence over time.

○ **Model correct usage and judiciously correct errors.** Use corrections to positively reinforce children's use of English. When English language learners make a mistake or use awkward language, they are often attempting to apply what they know about their first language to English. For example, a Spanish-speaking child may say, "It fell from me," a direct translation from Spanish, instead of "I dropped it."

○ **Use visual aids.** Present classroom content and information in a way that engages children—by using graphic organizers (word web, story maps, KWL charts), photographs, concrete materials, and graphs, for example.

Involving English Language Learners in Music Activities

Music is a universal language that draws people together. For English language learners, music can be a powerful vehicle for language learning and community-building. Music and singing are important to second language learners for many reasons, including:

○ The rhythms of music help children hear the sounds and intonation patterns of a new language.

○ Musical lyrics and accompanying motions help children learn new vocabulary.

○ Repetitive patterns of language in songs help children internalize the sentence structure of English.

○ Important cultural information is conveyed to young children in the themes of songs.

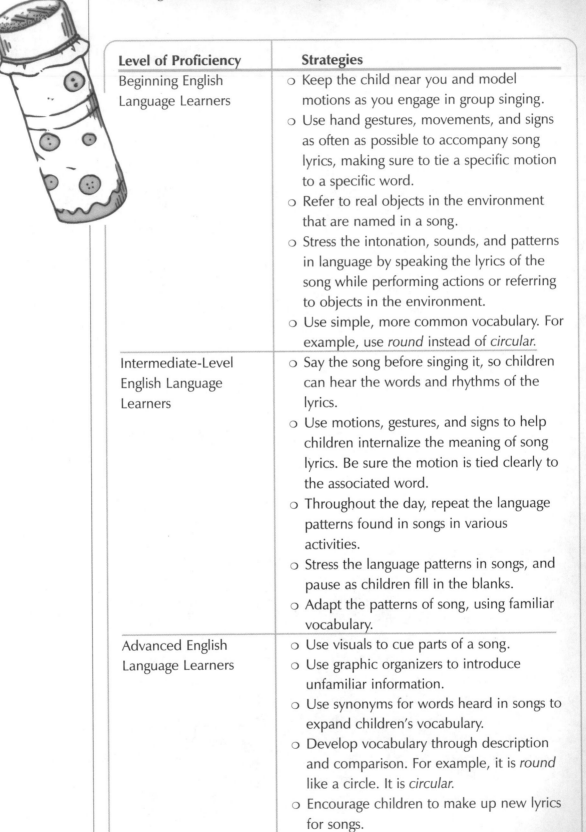

Strategies for involving English language learners in music activities vary according to the children's level of proficiency in the English language.

Level of Proficiency	Strategies
Beginning English Language Learners	o Keep the child near you and model motions as you engage in group singing. o Use hand gestures, movements, and signs as often as possible to accompany song lyrics, making sure to tie a specific motion to a specific word. o Refer to real objects in the environment that are named in a song. o Stress the intonation, sounds, and patterns in language by speaking the lyrics of the song while performing actions or referring to objects in the environment. o Use simple, more common vocabulary. For example, use *round* instead of *circular*.
Intermediate-Level English Language Learners	o Say the song before singing it, so children can hear the words and rhythms of the lyrics. o Use motions, gestures, and signs to help children internalize the meaning of song lyrics. Be sure the motion is tied clearly to the associated word. o Throughout the day, repeat the language patterns found in songs in various activities. o Stress the language patterns in songs, and pause as children fill in the blanks. o Adapt the patterns of song, using familiar vocabulary.
Advanced English Language Learners	o Use visuals to cue parts of a song. o Use graphic organizers to introduce unfamiliar information. o Use synonyms for words heard in songs to expand children's vocabulary. o Develop vocabulary through description and comparison. For example, it is *round* like a circle. It is *circular*. o Encourage children to make up new lyrics for songs.

How to Use This Book

Use the 25 songs on the *Bountiful Earth* CD (included with this book) and the related activities in this book to enhance themes in your curriculum, or use them independently. Either way you have a rich treasure chest of creative ideas for your classroom.

The eight-package collection provides more than 200 songs, a perfect combination of the traditional best-loved children's songs and brand-new selections created for each theme. Keep a song in your heart and put joy in your teaching!

Bibliography

Bulloch, K. 2003. *The mystery of modifying: Creative solutions.* Huntsville, TX: Education Service Center, Region VI.

Cavallaro, C. & M. Haney. 1999. *Preschool inclusion.* Baltimore, MD: Paul H. Brookes Publishing Company.

Gray, T. and S. Fleischman. Dec. 2004-Jan. 2005. "Research matters: Successful strategies for English language learners." *Educational Leadership,* 62, 84-85.

Hanniford, C. 1995. *Smart moves: Why learning is not all in your head.* Arlington, VA: Great Ocean Publications, p. 146.

LeDoux, J. 1993. "Emotional memory systems in the brain." *Behavioral and Brain Research,* 58.

Tabors, P. 1997. *One child, two languages: Children learning English as a second language.* Baltimore, MD: Paul H. Brookes Publishing Company.

Songs and Activities

I Love the Mountains

Chorus:
Boom-de-otta, boom-de-otta,
Boom-de-otta, boom-de-otta.
Boom-de-otta, boom-de-otta,
Boom-de-otta, boom-de-otta.

I love the mountains.
I love the rolling hills.
I love the flowers.
I love the daffodils.

(Chorus)

I love the rivers.
I love the winding streams.
I love the sunshine.
I love the moonlit beams.

(Chorus)
Boom!

Vocabulary

beam
daffodil
moonlight
mountain
river
rolling hills
stream

Theme Connections

Nature
Things I Like

Did You Know?

○ This song is a popular camp song. It can be sung in a round. If you sing it in a round, use only the first verse and the chorus.

○ There is not a universally accepted standard definition to differentiate between the height of a mountain and the height of a hill. A mountain, however, usually has an identifiable summit. The definition appears to change depending on geographic location.

○ All rivers run into the sea or the ocean. Streams and rivers are bodies of running water that are confined to channels and flow downhill under the influence of gravity. Streams that are more than 100 miles long are called rivers. Although this is the official difference between rivers and streams, the name is most often a local decision.

Literacy Links

Letter Knowledge

○ Print "Boom-de-otta" on a piece of chart paper. Discuss the letters in the word. *Which letters show up more than once? Which letter shows up most often?* Place the chart paper in the literacy center and provide magnetic letters. Invite the children to use the magnetic letters to copy the word.

Oral Language

- Discuss *boom-de-otta*. Explain that this is a nonsense word. It has no meaning. It is like "doodle-do" or "fiddle-i-fee." *Does it change the song if the word "doom-de-otta" is used instead of "boom-de-otta"? What about "zoom-de-otta"?* Sing the song using another nonsense word in place of boom-de-otta.
- Provide photos of daffodils. Encourage the children to describe the flower. Provide photos of mountains, rivers, streams, and hills. Use the photos to stimulate discussion.
- Teach the children to sign *love* using American Sign Language (page 120). If the children are interested, teach them the signs for *I*, *hill*, *mountain*, *flower*, and *stream*. Sing the song using the signs you have learned. This approach works well for English language learners.

Phonological Awareness

- *Boom* is an *onomatopoeic* word, a word that sounds like the sound it is describing. *What sound does it describe?* Name other *onomatopoeic* words that describe a loud noise (*wham*, *splat*).

Print Awareness/Oral Language

- Print "I love _____" on a sheet of chart paper. Encourage the children to fill in the blank. Discuss their answers. Try to write a song to same tune, using the children's words.

Curriculum Connections

Art

- Provide bright-colored paints and easel paper. Encourage the children to paint flowers.

Blocks

- Cut empty round cartons and empty paper towel tubes in half and place them around the floor to create hills. Provide small cars and encourage the children to travel up and down the hills.

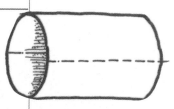

Fine Motor

- Provide clay and encourage the children to make a mountain or a hill. Have them use a toothpick to make a stream in their mountain. Place the mountains in the water table and slowly pour water over them. *Does the water run down the channel created for the stream?*

Book Corner

✓ **Special Needs Adaptation:** Making a mountain and a stream from clay can be used to encourage socialization and "peer buddy" interaction. Learning how to work with friends and knowing how to ask for help are important life skills. Assign the child with special needs a peer buddy, and have the children complete the activity together. Use words like *partner*, *team*, and *co-builders*, so the children realize it is a joint effort. Look for ways to help the child participate partially if she is unable to work on her own. For example, if a child does not have the fine motor skills to build a clay mountain, she may be able to help push clay up onto the mountain while her peer buddy molds it into a mountain.

Language
❍ Give the children a sentence starter, "I love _____." Challenge them to fill in the rest of the sentence, for example, "I love <u>playing outdoors</u>" or "I love <u>chocolate ice cream</u>." Write their full sentence on a sheet of paper. Encourage them to illustrate their sentence.

✓ **English Language Learner Strategy:** Provide pictures of things that appeal to children; for example, ice cream, books, balls, dolls, and balloons. Invite the children to complete the sentence by selecting one of the pictures.

Outdoors
❍ Show the children how to make mountains and hills in the sandbox. Make rivers by creating a trough in the sides of the mountains and hills. Add water and see where it runs.

Science
❍ Plant wildflower seeds in the fields and ditches close to the school or in an area of the playground that is not where the children typically play. Water as needed.

Social Studies
❍ Locate mountain ranges on a map or a globe. Locate rivers and streams.

Home Activities

❍ Have the children ask their family members which flower they like best.
❍ Suggest that the children bring a flower from their yard or their neighborhood to add to a classroom bouquet.

Down by the Bay

Vocabulary

bay
bear
bee
goose
hair
jig
knee
moose
polka dot
tail
watermelon
whale

Theme Connections

Family
Food/Nutrition
Make-Believe
Rhyming Words

Down by the bay
Where the watermelons grow,
Back to my home
I dare not go.
For if I do
My mother will say,
"Did you ever see a bear
Combing his hair
Down by the bay?"

Down by the bay
Where the watermelons grow,
Back to my home
I dare not go.
For if I do
My mother will say,
"Did you ever see a bee
With a sunburned knee
Down by the bay?"

Down by the bay
Where the watermelons grow,
Back to my home
I dare not go.
For if I do

My mother will say,
"Did you ever see a moose
Kissing a goose
Down by the bay?"

Down by the bay
Where the watermelons grow,
Back to my home
I dare not go.
For if I do
My mother will say,
"Did you ever see a whale
With a polka-dot tail
Down by the bay?"

Down by the bay
Where the watermelons grow,
Back to my home
I dare not go.
For if I do
My mother will say,
"Did you ever see a pig
Dancing the jig
Down by the bay?"

Did You Know?

❍ A bay is an indentation of a shoreline that is larger than a cove and smaller than a gulf.

❍ Watermelon is a fruit. Fruits are the edible parts of plants that have seeds. Vegetables, by contrast, are the edible parts of non-woody plants that do not have seeds. Tomatoes and peppers are often called vegetables but are actually fruits.

❍ Watermelons grow on a vine and must be replanted every year. They grow in sandy soil, and are about 90% water. Watermelons are part of the gourd family. They vary in shape and size.

Literacy Links

Phonological Awareness

○ Point out the rhyming pattern in the song. Have the children create new verses. Provide the first line of the *rhyming couplet*. For example, say, "Did you ever see a dog…" and let them come up with the second line.

✓ **Special Needs Adaptation:** A child with a significant language delay or a child with cognitive challenges will have difficulty with abstract concepts such as rhyming. They have difficulty generalizing or transferring information from one activity or concept to another. To help them understand the concept of rhyming, make flash cards. For example, print *moose* on one side of a card and put a picture of a moose above it. On the back of the card, print *goose* and a picture of a goose. Go over the cards with the child, flipping them back and forth. Ask him to repeat the words after you.

Print Awareness

○ Print a verse of the song on chart paper. Point out the quotation marks and question marks. Talk about how they are used in writing.

Letter Recognition/Phonological Awareness

○ Print the rhyming word pairs, for example, *pig/jig* and *moose/goose*, on chart paper. Have the children look at the words and determine which letter is different. Explain that the letter that is different is what changes the word and that words that are the same except for the beginning letter make *rhyming words*. If the children have had many experiences with rhyming word pairs, you might show them the rhyming word pair, *bear/hair*, where each word has several different letters but still rhymes.

Curriculum Connections

Art

○ Invite the children to draw whales with polka-dot tails.

Language

○ Give the children the "Down by the Bay" Rhyming Word Game (page 108). Help them match the rhyming pairs.

Math

○ Serve watermelon for snack. Have the children count the seeds they find.

Movement

○ Invite the children to make up a "Pig Jig."

Music and Movement

○ Dance the Hokey Pokey. Discuss the rhyming name of the dance.

 English Language Learner Strategy: Model the actions for the children until they are able to follow along with the song without assistance from you.

Science

○ Research locations where watermelons grow. *What kind of soil do they need to grow? How long does it take to grow from seed to fruit? How large do watermelons grow? How many kinds of watermelon are there?* If possible, visit a watermelon farm.

Social Studies

○ Display a map or a globe. Point out famous bays, such as Chesapeake Bay, Cape Cod Bay, and Biscayne Bay.

Home Activities

○ Send the words of the song home with children and have them ask their mother or another family member to respond to the line in the song, "My mother will say…." When the children bring their responses back to school, ask them to share them with the class.

○ Suggest that families look at a map with their child to find the closest bay. How far is the bay from their home?

Autumn Leaves Are Falling Down

by Pam Schiller

(Tune: London Bridge Is Falling Down)
Autumn leaves are falling down,
Falling down, falling down.
Autumn leaves are falling down,
Gently to the ground.

Autumn leaves are spinning round,
Spinning round, spinning round.
Autumn leaves are spinning round
In the autumn breeze.

Little children are dancing around,
Dancing around, dancing around.
Little children are dancing around
In the autumn leaves.

Vocabulary

autumn
breeze
dancing
falling
gently
spinning

Theme Connections

Autumn (fall)
Opposites
Seasons

Did You Know?

○ The range and intensity of autumn colors is greatly influenced by the weather. During autumn in the northern part of the United States, diminishing daylight hours and falling temperatures cause trees to prepare for winter by shedding billions of tons of leaves. This is preceded by a spectacular show of color. Formerly green leaves turn brilliant shades of yellow, orange, and red. These color changes are the result of transformations in leaf pigments.

○ Signs of autumn:
  1. Leaves change colors and fall off the trees.
  2. Weather becomes cooler.
  3. Days become shorter.
  4. Animals prepare for winter by growing thicker coats and storing food away.

○ Trees that drop their leaves in the fall are called deciduous trees. A maple tree loses about 600,000 leaves each fall.

○ The best place for viewing fall colors is the Eastern United States, particularly the New England states. The brightest colors are seen when a dry late summer is followed by bright sunny autumn days with cool nights (low 40's Fahrenheit). At these times, trees turn red, purple, and orange. A fall with cloudy days and warm nights produces drab colors, and an early frost quickly ends the colorful display. Fall leaves are generally at their peak in mid-October.

Literacy Links

Oral Language

○ Discuss the signs of autumn. Introduce the concept of two words describing the season, *autumn* and *fall*. Which word is familiar to the children?

○ Discuss autumn. *What are the signs of the season? Which colors are most visible? What kind of clothing do you wear? Which activities come with the season?*

○ Invite the children to dance like falling leaves. Have them spin, twirl, float, and dance.

Special Needs Adaptation: Children with autism spectrum disorder or autistic-like characteristics have difficulty understanding non-literal concepts. For example, the child understands that when she "falls down," she gets hurt. It will be very important that you make sure the child understands that the term "falling down" does not mean the leaves "get hurt." Don't be surprised if a child with Asperger's syndrome (a high-functioning type of autism) refuses to participate in the activity because she thinks you are "hurting the leaves when they fall down." Explain that the words "falling down" in the song really mean "coming off the trees." You might want to sing the song once, substituting the words "come off the trees" for "falling down."

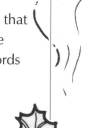

○ Teach the children the following fingerplay "Autumn Leaves Are Falling Down."

Autumn Leaves Are Falling Down
Autumn leaves are falling down,
Falling down, falling down. (wiggle fingers in downward motion)
Autumn leaves are falling down
Gently to the ground. (continue wiggling fingers until you touch the ground)

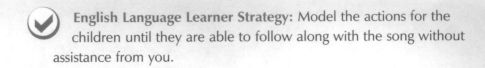 **English Language Learner Strategy:** Model the actions for the children until they are able to follow along with the song without assistance from you.

O Teach the children the "Falling Leaves" fingerplay.

> **Falling Leaves** by Pam Schiller
> *Little leaves are falling down,* (wiggle fingers downward)
> *Red and yellow, orange and brown.* (count on fingers)
> *Whirling, twirling round and round,* (twirl fingers)
> *Falling softly to the ground.* (wiggle finger downward to the ground)

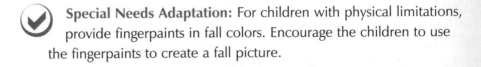 **Special Needs Adaptation:** Remember that children may interpret the concept of falling down literally. When they fall down they get hurt. *Do leaves get hurt when they fall down?* Demonstrate a leaf falling.

Print Awareness
O Encourage the children to write or dictate a new verse to the song.

Curriculum Connections

Art
O Encourage the children to gather leaves. Provide paper and glue so the children can make a leaf collage.
O Provide easel paper and red, yellow, brown, and orange tempera paint. Encourage the children to paint fall leaves and fall trees.

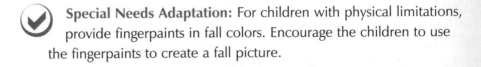 **Special Needs Adaptation:** For children with physical limitations, provide fingerpaints in fall colors. Encourage the children to use the fingerpaints to create a fall picture.

Discovery
O Invite children to make leaf rubbings. Have them place a leaf flat on the table and then place a sheet of tracing paper over the leaf. Use a crayon to gently rub over the tracing paper until the outline of the leaf shows through. Add other leaves and use different colors for a nice effect.

Fine Motor
O Provide playdough and leaf-shaped cookie cutters. Invite the children to cut leaf-shaped cookies.

Games

○ Invite the children to play Drop the Leaf. Provide a sack of leaves and a bucket. Have the children drop the leaf from chest level, attempting to get the leaf to drop into the bucket. *How many leaves land in the bucket? Why is it so difficult to accomplish?*

Language

○ Place a leaf on the tabletop. Encourage the children to blow the leaf off the table. Encourage them to describe the motions of the leaf as it falls to the floor. Provide larger and smaller leaves. *Does a large leaf fall differently than a smaller leaf?*

○ Provide pictures of fall foliage. Encourage the children to discuss the colors in the photos.

○ Make an "Autumn Leaf" book. Staple together five or six one-gallon-size resealable plastic bags at the bottom of the bags. Provide sheets of paper that fit inside the bags. Encourage the children to glue leaves to the sheets of paper. Transcribe their descriptions of the leaves onto each page; for example, "This leaf is small and red," "This leaf is large and orange," and so on. Make a cover sheet for the book.

staple

Math

○ Provide a stack of leaves and six paper sacks with the numerals 1-6 printed on them. Have the children count the correct number of leaves into each sack.

✔ **Special Needs Adaptation:** If six is too a high a number for the child to understand, use fewer sacks. For example, if a child has only worked with number concepts up to four, give her four sacks and extra time to count the leaves. After she gains understanding, add an additional sack. Allowing children to begin with a number they are comfortable with enhances competency without creating frustration.

○ Provide a pile of leaves. Encourage the children to sort the leaves in several different ways—by color, by size, and by shape.

✔ **Special Needs Adaptation:** Sort leaves into categories according to color. Ask the children how the leaves in each group are similar. Ask how the leaves in two groups are different. Sort the leaves a second time by size. Ask the children how the leaves in each stack are similar. Ask how the leaves in the two stacks are different.

Book Corner

Autumn Leaves by Ken Robbins

Every Autumn Comes the Bear by Jim Arnosky

I Know It's Autumn by Eileen Spinelli

Leaf Jumpers by Carole Gerber

Red Leaf, Yellow Leaf by Lois Ehlert

When Autumn Falls by Kelly Nidey

Music and Movement

○ Invite the children to move like falling leaves in a gusty wind. Have them move like falling leaves on a still day. Have them move like falling leaves in a rainstorm.

Science

○ Take an observation walk. *How many signs of fall/autumn can you find?* Make a list. Place a strip of masking tape turned sticky side out around each child's arm like a bracelet. Encourage the children to pick up fall leaves and stick them on their bracelets.

 Special Needs Adaptation: Assign children a partner to walk with. Have the partners work together to fill each bracelet with fallen leaves.

Social Studies

○ Discuss parts of the United States that enjoy colorful leaves during the fall/autumn. Discuss parts of the country where the leaves do not change colors or fall down. *Do the leaves in our area change colors and fall down?*

Writing

○ Print the color words *red, orange, yellow,* and *brown* on index cards. Write the words in the color of ink that matches the word. Provide tracing paper and encourage the children to trace over the letters of each word.

Home Activities

○ If children live in a location where fall leaves are abundant, suggest that they help their family rake and bag the leaves in their yards.

○ Ask children to bring a leaf from a tree in their neighborhood or yard. Have them glue or tape their leaf to a sheet of paper and print their name on the paper. Place the leaves in the science area and encourage the children to try to determine if any of the leaves come from the same kind of tree.

Down by the Old Mill Stream

Vocabulary

false
first
gingham
hate
love
mill
plaid
queen
second
stream
true
village

Theme Connections

Friendship
Nature
Opposites

Down by the old mill stream
Where I first met you
With your eyes so blue
Dressed in gingham, too.
It was there I knew
That I loved you true.
You were sixteen,
The village queen,
Down by the old mill stream.

Hit it! *(say this loudly, and then sing the rest of the song in a jazzy way)*
Down by the old (not the new, but the old)
Mill stream (not the river, but the stream)
Where I first (not second, but first)
Met you (not me, but you)
With your eyes (not your nose, but your eyes)
So blue (not green, but blue)
Dressed in gingham (not plaid, but gingham)
Too (not one, but two).
It was there (not here, but there)
I knew (not old, but knew)
That I loved (not hated, but loved)
You true (not false, but true).
You were sixteen (not seventeen, but sixteen),
The village queen (not the king, but the queen),
Down by the old (not the new, but the old)
Mill stream (not the river, but the stream).

Did You Know?

○ This song was written by Tell Taylor, who was from Ohio. "Down by the Old Mill Stream" was inspired by a spot on a river that flows through Findlay, Ohio.

○ "Down by the Old Mill Stream" is a popular barbershop quartet tune.

○ Rivers and streams are differentiated by their length. A channel of water that is longer than 100 miles is generally classified as a river. (See page 16 for more information about rivers and streams.)

○ A mill stream is a stream that runs beside a mill. A mill is a factory or a plant consisting of buildings with facilities that are used for manufacturing.

Literacy Links

Oral Language

○ Show the children a piece of gingham fabric. Ask them to describe the fabric. You may want to read "The Gingham Dog and the Calico Cat" by Eugene Field.

○ Discuss the play on words in the echo portion of the song. Which pairs of words are *opposites* (old/new, you/me, here/there), and which words are in a related family of words (sixteen/seventeen, queen/king, eyes/nose, first/second, green/blue, river/stream)?

> ✓ **Special Needs Adaptation:** Use this song to reinforce the concept of *opposites*. Make opposite word pair cards and practice them with the child. Go on an "opposite walk" with the child and encourage him to find opposite pairs of things. Use "opposite talk" throughout the day. For example, when you turn off the light say, "I am turning off the light; what is the opposite of *off*?" If the child says "on" say, "That is right" and turn the light on. If he does not answer, turn the light on and say, "*On* is the opposite of *off*."

○ Discuss words in the song that may be new vocabulary; for example, *mill*, *gingham*, *stream*, *river*, and other words that are new to the children.

> ✓ **English Language Learner Strategy:** Provide pictures of the words so the children will better understand their meaning.

Curriculum Connections

Art

○ Provide scraps of gingham and plaid material. Invite the children to make a collage with the fabric. Discuss the differences in the fabrics. *Do all plaids look alike? Do all ginghams look alike?*

Dramatic Play

○ Provide props such as crowns, robes, thrones, and scepters for children to play king and queen.

Language

○ Encourage the children to sort blue and green items or old and new items.

 Special Needs Adaptation: Pair children with peer buddies and ask them to work as a team to sort the items.

Listening

○ Provide barbershop quartet music for the children to enjoy.

Math

○ Provide buttons, beads, paper clips, and other objects to count. Challenge the children to count 16 of each item and put them into containers. Do *16 buttons take up the same amount of space in the jar as 16 paper clips?*

Special Needs Adaptation: Count 16 beads, buttons, and paper clips each into separate jars. Ask the children which jar appears to contain the most items. Dump the items out of each jar and lay them in rows that demonstrate a one-to-one correspondence. Help the children determine that the number of items in each jar is the same and that it is only the size of the item that makes one jar appear fuller than another.

Book Corner

Math/Social Studies

○ Make a graph of eye colors represented in the classroom. Have the children look in a mirror to verify their eye color and then place a marker on the graph to represent the color of their eyes. *How many children have the same color eyes mentioned in the song?*

Social Studies

○ Find Findlay, Ohio on a map. *What river runs through Findlay?* Tell the children that this is the stream that inspired the song "Down by the Old Mill Stream."

Water Play

○ Provide a shallow tub of water and large rocks and clay so the children can section off the water to make a stream or a river.

Home Activity

○ Encourage the children to see if they can find gingham material in their homes. Suggest that they check clothing, tablecloths, napkins, towels, and furniture coverings.

The Green Grass Grew All Around

Vocabulary

around
bird
branch
egg
grass
green
hole
nest
park
prettiest

Theme Connections

Animals
Colors
Growing Things
Nature

In the park
There was a hole.
Oh, the prettiest hole
You ever did see!
A hole in the park,
And the green grass grew
All around, all around,
And the green grass grew all around.

And in that hole
There grew a tree.
Oh, the prettiest tree
You ever did see!
Tree in the hole,
Hole in the park,
And the green grass grew
All around, all around,
And the green grass grew all around.

And on that tree
There was a branch.
Oh, the prettiest branch
You ever did see!
Branch on the tree,
Tree in the hole,
Hole in the park,
And the green grass grew
All around, all around,
And the green grass grew all around.

And on that branch
There was a nest.
Oh, the prettiest nest
You ever did see!
Nest on the branch,
Branch on the tree,
Tree in the hole,

Hole in the park,
And the green grass grew
All around, all around,
And the green grass grew all around.

And in that nest
There was an egg.
Oh, the prettiest egg
You ever did see!
Egg in the nest,
Nest on the branch,
Branch on the tree,
Tree in the hole,
Hole in the park,
And the green grass grew
All around, all around,
And the green grass grew all around.

And on that egg
There was a bird.
Oh, the prettiest bird
You ever did see!
Bird on the egg,
Egg in the nest,
Nest on the branch,
Branch on the tree,
Tree in the hole,
Hole in the park,
And the green grass grew
All around, all around,
And the green grass grew all around.
And the green grass grew
All around, all around,
And the green grass grew all around.

Did You Know?

○ "The Green Grass Grew All Around" is cumulative text and uses predictable language. It is also an echo song, which means children repeat each line after it is sung.

○ During the breeding season, a nest is the environment in which birds' eggs develop. Some birds do not build nests, but instead lay their eggs directly on the ground, in a hole, or even on a bare branch. Other birds' nests are elaborate works of architecture.

○ Nest size, shape, and building materials vary greatly. The placement and design of nests provide protection from temperature extremes and from predators. Birds instinctively know how to build a nest that is characteristic of their particular species.

○ Woodpeckers excavate their nests in tree trunks or branches. These nest cavities offer safety from predators and a comfortable microclimate for their eggs and their young.

Literacy Links

Oral Language

○ Have the children make up a last verse about what is in the egg that the bird is sitting on.

Phonological Awareness/Letter Knowledge

○ Print "green grass grew" on chart paper. Ask the children to identify the first two letters in each word. Say the phrase slowly. Ask the children if they hear a repetitive sound at the beginning of each word. Can someone reproduce the sound that he or she hears? It is not important that the children connect the sound to the blend of /gr/ but they should be able to hear the repetitive sound. Point out that the repetition of beginning sounds in a phrase or a sentence is called *alliteration*.

Curriculum Connections

Art

○ Provide paintbrushes, easel paper, and green tempera paint. Encourage the children to paint green grass pictures.

○ Draw a tree trunk and branches on a large piece of white butcher paper and then paint it. Provide sponges and green tempera paint. Invite the children to use the sponges to make leaf prints on the tree branches. It is not necessary to cut sponges into leaf shapes because the sponges will provide a lacey look that simulates the way trees look at a distance.

Construction

○ Provide grass, hay, dried leaves, and coffee filters. Invite the children to glue the grass, hay, and leaves onto the filter to create a bird's nest.

Cooking

○ Invite the children to make candy bird nests. Melt a bag of butterscotch chips in the microwave. Add Chow Mein noodles and mix until the noodles are all coated. Have the children scoop spoonfuls of the mixture and drop them on wax paper. Show them how to press their spoons into the centers of the dropped mixture to create bird's nests. Allow to cool before serving.

Math

○ Fill plastic eggs with objects of different weights. Challenge the children to organize the eggs from the heaviest to the lightest, "weighing" the eggs by holding them in their hands.

Music

○ Give the children paper plates to use for wings and encourage them to fly like birds to classical music.

✓ **Special Needs Adaptation:** It may be difficult for children with limited motor skills to participate in activities that require diverse movements. Adapt the paper plates with pipe cleaner handles on each paper plate. Make a loop with the pipe cleaner and twist the bottoms together. Insert the pipe cleaner into the center of the plate through a small hole and tape it down. The child can use the loop as a handle for holding the plate. Another alternative is to make a Velcro bracelet for the child to place around his palm. Attach a piece of Velcro to the plate and have the child attach the plate to his bracelet. He can move with the music without being concerned about holding on to the plate.

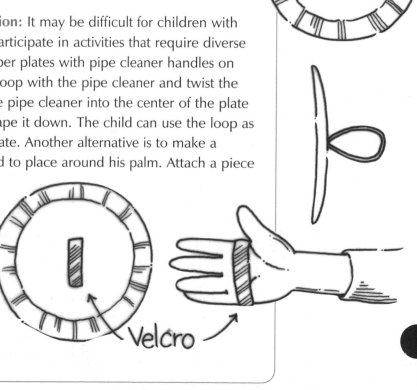

Velcro

Book Corner

Are You My Mother?
by P.D. Eastman
Baby Bird's First Nest
by Frank Asch
*There Was an Old
Lady Who
Swallowed a Fly*
by Simms Taback
*This Is the House
That Jack Built* by
Simms Taback

Science

○ Locate a real bird's nest and place it in the science center for observation. If a real nest cannot be found, provide photos of birds' nests.

○ Provide leaves, paper, and crayons. Encourage the children to make leaf rubbings.

Writing

○ Provide feathers, small branches, and tempera paint. Show the children how to use the feathers and the branches as writing tools by dipping them into the paint. Encourage the children to write their names or draw pictures.

Home Activity

○ Encourage the children to count the trees in their yards. Many will have no trees, which is fine. Make a graph that shows how many trees children have in their yard.

Johnny Appleseed

Vocabulary

apple seed
earth
fruit
shade
thank
tree

Theme Connections

Folktales
Fruits
Growing Things

Oh, the Earth is good to me,
And so I thank the Earth,
For giving me the things I need—
The sun, and the rain, and the apple seed.
The Earth is good to me.

Oh, apples are good for me,
And so I thank the tree,
For giving me the fruit I need—
The fruit, the shade, and the apple seed.
The tree is good to me.

Did You Know?

○ This song was originally spoken as a grace at mealtimes. It is often used today as a song about the bountiful earth.
○ The real Johnny Appleseed was John Chapman; he was born on September 26, 1774 near Leominster, Massachusetts. By the time he was 25 years old, he had become a nurseryman and had planted apple trees in the western portions of New York and Pennsylvania. Some of the present-day orchards in those areas are said to have originated with his apple trees.
○ Apples come in all shades of red, green, and yellow.
○ A medium apple is about 80 calories.
○ Apples are grown in all 50 states.

Literacy Links

Comprehension

○ Read the listening story "Johnny Appleseed" (page 105). Ask the children to close their eyes and to imagine the pictures that might go with this story.

o   Invite the children to re-enact "Tiny Seed."

Tiny Seed

Tiny seed planted just right, (children tuck themselves into a ball)
Not a breath of air, not a ray of light.
Rain falls slowly to and fro,
And now the seed begins to grow. (children begin to unfold)
Slowly reaching for the light,
With all its energy, all its might.
The little seed's work is almost done,
To grow up tall and face the sun. (children stand up tall with arms stretched overhead)

 English Language Learner Strategy: Model the actions for the children until they are able to follow along on their own.

Letter Knowledge

o   Print *apple* on chart paper. Discuss the letters in the word. *What letter does* apple *start with? Which letters appear more than once?*

Special Needs Adaptation: Touching the letters helps a child learn more about that letter. Use large raised letters or magnetic letters and encourage the child to trace each letter with her fingers as you spell the word and say the letter for her. For a child with a hearing loss, remember to teach the finger sign for each new letter that you introduce. (See page 122 for alphabet finger signs.)

Oral Language

o   Show the children an apple. Point out the stem and the skin. Cut the apple in half. Point out the location of the seeds. Mention that the white part of the apple is called the meat. Cut an apple in half horizontally and show the star inside the apple to the children.

Oral Language/Comprehension

o   Teach the children the following apple fingerplays.

Little Red Apple

A little red apple grew high in a tree. (point up)
I looked up at it. (shade eyes and look up)
It looked down at me. (shade eyes and look down)
"Come down, please," I called. (use hand to motion downward)
And that little red apple fell right on my head. (tap the top of your head)

My Apple

Look at my apple, it is nice and round. (cup hands)
It fell from a tree, down to the ground. (move fingers in a
    downward motion)
Come, let me share my apple, please do! (beckoning motion)
My mother can cut it in two— (slicing motion)
One half for me and one half for you. (hold out two hands,
    sharing halves)

 English Language Learner Strategy: Model the actions for the children until they are able to follow along on their own.

Curriculum Connections

Art
○ Cut easel paper into apple shapes. Provide red, green, and yellow paint and encourage each child to paint an apple.

Cooking
○ Invite the children to make applesauce. Peel, core, and cut up 6 apples into a large saucepan. Add ½ cup water, 1 teaspoon lemon juice, and ¼ cup sugar. Cook until tender. Add a pinch of cinnamon. Press through a colander and serve. **Note**: Check for allergies before serving.

Discovery
○ Give the children a ball to roll and an apple to roll. Make a 3' line on the floor with masking tape and challenge the children to roll each item down the line. *Which item is more difficult to roll? Why?* **Note:** Ask the children to treat the apple gently because it will be used for snack.

Dramatic Play
○ Provide props, such as a pot for a hat, wood for a campfire, a knapsack, overalls, and a walking stick, for the children to use to pretend to be Johnny Appleseed.

Fine Motor
○ Provide tweezers to transfer apple seeds from one cup to another cup.

 Special Needs Adaptation: Provide apple seeds, a pastry brush, and a plastic cup. Encourage the children to use the pastry brush to sweep the seeds from the tabletop into the cup.

Games

○ Play Fruit Basket Turn Over. Sit in a circle; select one child to stand in the center. Assign the name of a fruit to each child. The child in the center of the circle calls out the name of two fruits. The two children who were assigned the names of those fruits must quickly change seats. The child in the middle also tries to reach one of the seats. The one left standing then calls the name of two other fruits. This child may also call out "fruit basket turn over," and then everyone must change seats.

Math

○ Provide red, yellow, and green apple slices for snack. Encourage the children to try each color of apple and then vote for the color they liked best. Show them how to mark their choice on a graph. Analyze the results of their choices. Do more children like red, green, or yellow apples? Which color apple do the least number of children like?

Special Needs Adaptation: Provide 4" squares of construction paper in yellow, green, and red. Have the children select a square that is the same color as the apple they liked best. Arrange the squares on the floor to create a graph.

Apple Chart

Children	Red Apple	Yellow Apple	Green Apple
Kelly			■
Brian	■		
Jacob		■	
Arron	■		
Damon			■
Tasha		■	
Lizabeth	■		
Jeffrey		■	
Adam	■		
Micah		■	
Brittney		■	
Marcus		■	
Kevin		■	

Apples and Pumpkins
by Anne
Rockwell
Apples Here by Will
Hubbell
Johnny Appleseed by
Reeve Lindbergh
Johnny Appleseed by
Steven Kellogg

Science

○ Allow children to watch the transformation of an apple as it ripens over time. Show the children an apple when it is fresh. Discuss the texture, color, shape, and size of the apple. Examine the apple again every couple of days. When the apple begins to get soft, place it on a plate and continue to pass it around the circle and encourage the children to touch it lightly. Discuss the changes in the apple each time you look at it. When the apple has become really mushy, place it outdoors for the birds and other animals to eat and enjoy!

○ Give the children the Seed-to-Fruit sequence cards (page 107). Have them arrange the cards in order from seed to fruit. Discuss the stages of the growth of a seed into a tree with fruit.

✓ **Special Needs Adaptation:** Have the children work with a peer buddy. Suggest that the buddy arrange the cards in a sequence and that the second child state whether the sequence correctly shows the steps from seed to fruit.

Home Activity

○ Suggest that children look at home for apples or things that are made from apples, such as jelly, pies, cookies, and juices.

Mister Moon

Oh, Mister Moon, Moon,
Bright and shiny moon,
Won't you please shine down on me?
Oh, Mister Moon, Moon,
Bright and shiny moon,
Won't you please set me fancy free?
I'd like to linger, but I've got to run,
Mama's callin',
"Baby, get your homework done!"
Oh, Mister Moon, Moon,
Bright and shiny moon,
Won't you please shine down on,
Talk about your shine on,
Please shine down on me!
Oh yeah!

Vocabulary

down
fancy
fancy free
homework
linger
moon
shine
shiny

Theme Connections

Day and Night
Nature

Did You Know?

○ Our moon is bigger than the planet Pluto. And at roughly one-fourth the diameter of Earth, some scientists think the moon is more like a planet. They refer to the Earth-moon system as a "double planet."

○ The moon is an egg shape, not round. The big end of the egg faces earth.

○ It would take 135 days driving 70 miles an hour to drive to the moon (if it was possible to drive to the moon). It takes 60 to 70 hours to fly to the moon in a rocket.

○ The moon rises each night 50 minutes later than it rose the day before.

○ The new moon always rises at sunrise and the first quarter moon at noon. The full moon always rises at sunset and the last quarter moon at midnight.

○ The moon controls the ocean tides. The moon's gravity pulls on Earth's oceans. High tide aligns with the moon as the Earth spins underneath the moon. Another high tide occurs on the opposite side of the planet because the pull of gravity pulling Earth toward the moon is greater than the pull of gravity pulling the water toward the moon.

Literacy Links

Oral Language
○ Discuss the new vocabulary in the song; for example, *fancy free* and *linger*.
○ Teach the children the American Sign Language sign for *moon* (page 120).

Oral Language
○ Talk about the moon. Make a KWL chart using the pattern on page 119. The chart has three columns: What I Know, What I Want to Know, and What I Learned. Ask children what they know about the moon and fill in the information on the chart. Ask what they would like to know and fill that in on the chart. After you have studied the moon and provided the information that children would like to know, you will be able to fill in the last column.

Letter Knowledge/Phonological Awareness
○ Print "Mister Moon, Moon" on chart paper. Underline the first letter in each word and ask the children to identify the first letters. Have the children say "Mister Moon, Moon" slowly. Ask the children if they can hear the /m/ sound at the beginning of each word. Explain that repetition of a beginning sound in several words in a row is called *alliteration*.

Curriculum Connections

Art
○ Provide black construction paper and white chalk. Invite the children to draw night sky pictures.

✔ **Special Needs Adaptation:**
Provide lap-size flannel boards made by gluing black felt to squares of cardboard. Cut out moons in all phases and several sizes of stars from white felt. Encourage the children to place the cutouts on their flannel boards to create a night sky.

Book Corner

Fireflies by Julie Brinckloe

Goodnight Moon by Margaret Wise Brown

Grandfather Twilight by Barbara Berger

Night in the Country by Cynthia Rylant

Owl Moon by Jane Yolen

Discovery

○ Cut moons and stars from white poster board. Challenge the children to roll the stars and the moons. *Which items roll? Which items do not roll?*

Games

○ Play Moonbeam Shadows. Hang a sheet from the floor to the ceiling. Place a bright light, such as an overhead projector, behind the sheet. Divide the class in half. Half of the class are the audience (they guess who the performers are) and the other half are the performers. Seat the audience in front of the sheet. Send the performers one at a time behind the sheet to do something silly; for example, strike a pose, dance, and so on. Challenge the audience to identify the performer.

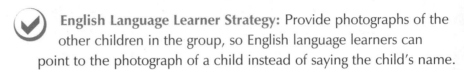 **English Language Learner Strategy:** Provide photographs of the other children in the group, so English language learners can point to the photograph of a child instead of saying the child's name.

Listening

○ Play lullaby music for the children. Encourage them to select a favorite lullaby.

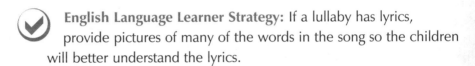 **English Language Learner Strategy:** If a lullaby has lyrics, provide pictures of many of the words in the song so the children will better understand the lyrics.

Math

○ Cut white construction paper into quarter moons, half moons, three-quarter moons, and full moons. Challenge the children to arrange the moon in its cycle from new moon to full moon and then from full moon to new.

Music

○ Provide white crepe paper streamers. Play classical music and invite the children to dance like moonbeams.

Science

○ Provide photographs of the moon and stars. If available, show the children a telescope.

Home Activity

○ Suggest that families go outside on a clear night to enjoy the night sky with their children. Ask them to note the stage of the moon and the brightness or dullness of the stars.

Winter Is Coming

Vocabulary

bare
bundle
button
coat
cold
darker
mitten
snowflake
tongue
tree
wind

Theme Connections

Seasons
Winter

by Pam Schiller

(Tune: London Bridge Is Falling Down)
Can you feel the wind blow cold,
Wind blow cold,
Wind blow cold?
Can you feel the wind blow cold?
Winter's coming soon.

Can you see the darker skies,
Darker skies,
Darker skies?
Can you see the darker skies?
Winter's coming soon.

Can you see the trees are bare,
Trees are bare,
Trees are bare?
Can you see the trees are bare?
Winter's coming soon.

Time to button up your coat,
Put your mittens on,
And bundle up.
Catch a snowflake on your tongue.
Winter time is here!

Did You Know?

○ Winter is one of the four seasons in temperate zones. Winter begins with the winter solstice (December 21 in the northern hemisphere and June 21 in the southern hemisphere), and ends with the spring equinox (March 21 in the northern hemisphere and September 21 in the southern hemisphere). Sometimes it is counted as the months of June, July, and August in the southern hemisphere and December, January, and February in the northern hemisphere.

○ Winter terms: Hail is a chunk or stone of ice dropped during a thunderstorm. Sleet is frozen rain. Freezing rain is liquid rain that freezes when it fall on surfaces, such as a road or tree.

o Snow is created when water freezes inside clouds and forms ice crystals. Ice crystals form around tiny bits of dirt that have been carried up into the atmosphere by the wind. These ice crystals join together to create snowflakes. Once the flakes are heavy enough, they fall to the ground as snow.

o Most snowflakes are smaller than one-half inch across. The largest snowflake recorded was 15 inches in diameter. All snowflakes have six sides; no two snowflakes are alike.

Literacy Links

Oral Language

o Make a Word Web (page 118) for winter. Start by writing *winter* in the center of a sheet of chart paper. Draw a circle around it. Ask the children to tell you what they know about winter and write their responses on lines drawn around *winter*.

> **Special Needs Adaptation:** Print *cold* on chart paper and encourage children to name things that are cold. Prompt children with limited communication skills by holding up a picture of something cold and asking, "Is this cold?" Alternate using pictures of things that are cold with pictures of things that are hot. This teaches children to discriminate between *hot* and *cold*.

Phonological Awareness

o Write *cold* on chart paper. Ask the children to think of words that rhyme with "cold," for example, *hold*, *told*, *sold*, *bold*, and *gold*.

Print Awareness

o Make a list of things mentioned in the song that are conditions of winter, such as cold wind, bare trees, and darker skies. Have the children look out the window to notice any signs of winter and check things on the list that they can see or feel. Teach them to put the palm of their hands on the windowpane to determine how cold it is outside.

> **English Language Learner Strategy:** Create or purchase pictures of winter conditions that have the descriptive word written under them. Give these pictures to a child and ask him or her to look out the window for similar winter conditions.

Curriculum Connections

Art
○ Prepare Puff Paint. Mix ⅓ cup white glue, 2 tablespoons white tempera paint, and 2 cups shaving cream. Provide blue construction paper. Invite the children to use the Puff Paint as fingerpaint, and suggest that they paint snowy day pictures.

Discovery
○ Freeze a small toy inside a block of ice. Place the block of ice on a plate and encourage the children to watch it melt. *Are there things you can do to make it melt more quickly? What would happen if you placed it by the heater or in a sunny window? What would happen if you blow on it or fan it?*

Dramatic Play
○ Provide a variety of winter clothing and a mirror. Encourage the children to experiment with everything from sweaters and coats to mittens and socks. *How are winter clothes different from the clothing worn in other seasons?*

Fine Motor
○ Make Snow Dough. Mix 1 cup flour, ½ cup salt, 1 cup water, 2 tablespoons vegetable oil, 1 tablespoon cream of tartar, ½ teaspoon clear glitter, and ½ cup white tempera paint. Cook over medium heat, stirring until a ball is formed. Knead the dough until cool.

 English Language Learner Strategy: Use a rebus (page 116) for this recipe to make it easier for the children to follow the directions.

Science
○ Take the children on a nature walk to look for signs of winter. When you return to the classroom, make a list of the signs of winter you saw on your walk.

Snack
○ Serve hot chocolate for snack. Invite children to put their own marshmallow in the chocolate.

Home Activity

○ Encourage the children to notice things they can see at home that might indicate that winter is coming. Are their summer clothes being put away? Is the furnace being turned on? Are the trees around their homes losing their leaves or are they bare of leaves?

I Made a Pumpkin

I made a pumpkin yellow.
I gave it two round eyes.
Cut a circle for the nose
And a funny mouth that smiles.
Then I hide behind the bush,
Wait until it's dark.
Then when Daddy comes along,
Out I jump.
"Boo!" I shout.
What a surprise!

Vocabulary

bush
circle
eyes
funny
jump
pumpkin
round
smile
surprise
yellow

Did You Know?

○ Pumpkins grow on vines.
○ Pumpkins are used to make soups, pies, and breads. Pumpkin seeds can be roasted as a snack. Pumpkin flowers are edible.
○ Pumpkins range in size from less than a pound to over 1,000 pounds. The largest pumpkin ever grown weighed 1,140 pounds.
○ Pumpkins are 90% water, and contain potassium and Vitamin A.
○ Pumpkins are fruit. Fruits are edible parts of plants that have seeds inside. Vegetables, by contrast, are edible parts of non-woody plants that have no seeds.

Theme Connections

Colors
Growing Things
Halloween

Literacy Links

Letter Knowledge

○ Print *boo* on chart paper. Discuss the letters. *What letter does* boo *start with? What other letters are in "boo?"*

Oral Language

○ Write question marks all over a large box to make it a mystery box. Place a pumpkin inside. Provide clues and encourage the children to guess what is inside the box.

- How is *boo* used in the song? What other sounds are used to frighten people (screams, growls, roars)?
- Discuss Halloween safety. In addition to discussing Halloween safety, talk about other safety rules, such as never going anywhere with strangers and learning to walk away if someone makes fun of you.

Phonological Awareness
- Teach children the fingerplay, "Five Little Pumpkins."

Five Little Pumpkins
Five little pumpkins sitting on a gate. (hold up five fingers)
First one said, "It's getting late." (wiggle first finger)
Second one said, "There's witches in the air." (wiggle second finger)
Third one said, "We don't care." (wiggle third finger)
Fourth one said, "Let's run and run and run." (wiggle fourth finger)
Fifth one said, "Oh, it's just Halloween fun." (wiggle fifth finger)
But whooo went the wind and out went the light, (place hands sides on your cheeks and blow)
And five little pumpkins rolled out of sight. (roll hand over hand)

 English Language Learner Strategy: Model the actions for the children until they are able to follow along independently.

Curriculum Connections

Art
- Help children place 1 tablespoon pumpkin seeds and 1 tablespoon orange tempera paint inside a potato chip can. Roll a sheet of art paper to fit inside the can. Invite the children to shake the can to create a pumpkin-seed design on their papers.

Construction
- Create a pumpkin patch. Provide small- and medium-size paper lunch bags. Have the children stuff the bags with wadded newspaper until they are three-quarters full. Tie off the top of the bag with green pipe cleaners. Provide orange and green tempera paint for the children to use to paint the pumpkins and the stems. Group the pumpkins on the floor to create a pumpkin patch.
- Help the children carve a pumpkin.

Discovery

❍ Invite the children to color a coffee filter with yellow and orange crayons. When they have finished, help them fold the coffee filter into a wedge and then dip the wide edge in a cup of water. Have them take the filter out of the water and rotate it so the water spreads throughout the filter. *What happens when the water spreads?*

Field Trip

❍ Visit a pumpkin farm.

Fine Motor

❍ Make Pumpkin Playdough. Mix 5½ cups flour, 2 cups salt, 8 teaspoons cream tartar, ¾ cup vegetable oil, one container of pumpkin pie spice (1½ ounces), orange food coloring (mix red and yellow), and 4 cups water. Cook and stir over medium heat until smooth. Remove from the pot and knead on a floured surface until the mixture is the consistency of playdough. Encourage the children to smell the dough as they play with it.

Gross Motor

❍ Roll a pumpkin across the floor. Encourage the children to roll like pumpkins.

✔ **Special Needs Adaptation:** Provide a ball to use for a pumpkin. Encourage the children to roll the ball. Have them make a circle with their arms. Provide a real pumpkin. Have the children roll the pumpkin. *Which rolls easier, the ball or the pumpkin?*

Language

❍ Divide a sheet of copy paper into six equal sections. In each square, draw a jack-o-lantern, each with a different face. Make two copies of your drawings on card stock. Cut the sections apart to make a set of matching cards. Invite the children to match the faces. You can control the difficulty by making the faces more or less different.

Book Corner

Science

○ Prepare six cards (4" x 6" index cards work well) that illustrate the stages of a pumpkin's life cycle: seed, sprout, plant, flower, green pumpkin, and orange pumpkin. Encourage the children to arrange the cards in order to show the growth of a pumpkin from seed to fruit.

Snack

○ Make Pumpkin Milkshakes. Blend 2 cups vanilla ice cream, ½ cup milk, and 4 tablespoons pumpkin pie filling in a blender. Serves four.

 English Language Learner Strategy: Use a rebus (page 115) for this recipe to make it easier to follow the directions.

Home Activity

○ Send a paper bag Jack-o-Lantern home with each child, and ask each child to work with his or her family to think of a creative name for the Jack-o-Lantern.

When I'm Chilly

by Pam Schiller

(Tune: Mary Had a Little Lamb)
When I'm chilly through and through,
Through and through,
Through and through,
When I'm chilly through and through,
Give me soup or stew.

When the heat is hard to beat,
Hard to beat,
Hard to beat,
When the heat is hard to beat,
Give me ice cream—what a treat!

Vocabulary

chilly
hard to beat
heat
soup
stew
through
treat

Theme Connections

Clothing
Seasons
Winter

Did You Know?

○ Several suggestions for staying warm on a chilly day include eating warm soup, drinking hot chocolate, exercising, and bundling up, especially the head, hands, and feet.

○ Going outside (even in cold weather) for at least 30 minutes can have a positive impact on one's mood.

○ Taking a trip to someplace warm in the middle of winter or lingering outside when spring arrives can improve mood, memory, and creative thinking (Keller, 2004).

○ See more cold weather facts on page 87 in "Cap, Mittens, Boots, and Scarf."

Literacy Links

Oral Language

○ Discuss ways to stay warm on a cold day. Make a list of the children's ideas on chart paper. Discuss ways to stay cool on a hot day. Make a list of the children's ideas on chart paper. Compare the lists.

○ Share the listening story, "The Wind and the Sun" (page 106), with the children. Encourage them to create their own illustrations for the story by using their imaginations.

○ Display winter photos. Use the photos to stimulate conversation about winter. *How do you know the weather is cold?* Display summer photos. Use the photos to stimulate conversation about summer. *How do you know the weather is warm?*

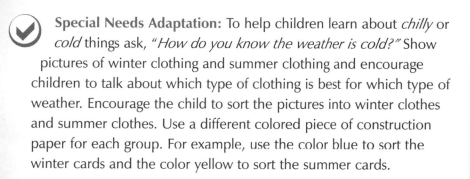 **Special Needs Adaptation:** To help children learn about *chilly* or *cold* things ask, *"How do you know the weather is cold?"* Show pictures of winter clothing and summer clothing and encourage children to talk about which type of clothing is best for which type of weather. Encourage the child to sort the pictures into winter clothes and summer clothes. Use a different colored piece of construction paper for each group. For example, use the color blue to sort the winter cards and the color yellow to sort the summer cards.

Curriculum Connections

Art

○ As the ice is forming in an ice tray, place craft sticks into each cube to create ice brushes. Provide dry tempera paint and paper. Invite the children to sprinkle dry tempera on their papers and then paint with their ice brushes.

○ Provide a sheet of drawing paper and crayons. Encourage the children to draw a warm weather picture on one side of their paper and a cool weather picture on the other side.

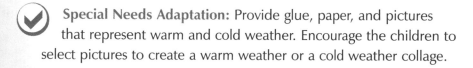 **Special Needs Adaptation:** Provide glue, paper, and pictures that represent warm and cold weather. Encourage the children to select pictures to create a warm weather or a cold weather collage.

Cooking

○ Invite the children to help make Baggie Ice Cream. Mix ½ cup milk, 1 tablespoon sugar, and ¼ teaspoon vanilla in a small resealable plastic bag and close the bag. Place the small bag inside a large resealable plastic bag of ice and add 3 tablespoons rock salt. Close and shake. The mixture will freeze in 10 to 15 minutes.

 English Language Learner Strategy: Use a rebus (page 111) for this recipe to make it easier to follow the directions.

Book Corner

Fox Tale Soup by
  Tony Bonning
The Mitten by Jan
  Brett
*Right Outside My
  Window* by Mary
  Ann Hoberman
The Snowy Day by
  Ezra Jack Keats
Stone Soup by
  Marcia Brown
Winter's Tale by
  Robert Sabuda

Discovery

❍ Provide pictures of outdoor activities, people dressed in warm or cold clothing, and animals that are seen during warm or cold weather. Encourage the children to sort the photos into warm and cold categories.

Dramatic Play

❍ Provide props for making soup, such as a pot, plastic vegetables, cups, and spoons. Encourage the children to pretend to make soup.

❍ Provide winter and summer clothing. Invite the children to sort the clothing.

Science

❍ Teach the children how to rub their hands together to keep them warm. Discuss friction and its by-product—heat.

Snack

❍ Invite the children to help prepare hot chocolate. Don't forget the marshmallows!

Home Activity

❍ Have the children ask family members to name their favorite wintertime food and their favorite summertime food.

Earth Is Our Home

Vocabulary

animal
clean
Earth
home
keep
people

Theme Connections

Animals
Environment
Nature

by Beverly Irby and Rafael Lara-Alecio

(Tune: The Farmer in the Dell)
Earth is our home.
Earth is our home.
For people and for animals,
Earth is our home.

Let's keep our home clean.
Let's keep our home clean.
For people and for animals,
Let's keep our home clean.

Earth is our home.
Earth is our home.
For people and for animals,
Earth is our home.

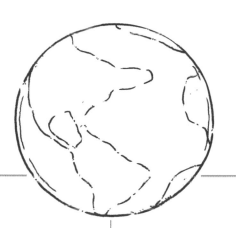

Did You Know?

○ More than 6 billion people live on the planet Earth.
○ Despite being called Earth, only 29% of the surface is actually "earth," 71% is made up of water.
○ Seen from outer space, Earth would be the brightest of the nine planets. This is because sunlight is reflected by the planet's water.
○ Our oceans are polluted by many things, including trash, oil from ships, and fertilizers that run off farmland into rivers and streams and eventually into the ocean.
○ Earth's land is also polluted by many things, including litter and pesticides. Litter is trash, wastepaper, or garbage that is not in garbage or trash cans.
○ Endangered species are animals that are in danger of becoming extinct. Once a species disappears or becomes extinct, it is gone forever.

Literacy Links

Oral Language

○ Define and discuss the planet Earth. Display a simple picture of our solar system. Point out Earth, the sun, and the moon. Show the children a globe. Make the connection between the two-dimensional picture of

Earth and the three-dimensional globe. Show the children where they live. Explain that people and animals live on the many land areas on the globe. Remind them that many animals and some people, such as those who live on houseboats and on ships, also live on water.

❍ Teach the children the America Sign Language sign for *earth* (page 120).

❍ Teach the children the poem "I'm Glad the Sky Is Painted Blue."

> **I'm Glad the Sky Is Painted Blue**
> *I'm glad the sky is painted blue,*
> *And the earth is painted green.*
> *With such a lot of nice fresh air*
> *All sandwiched in between.*

Print Awareness

❍ Help the children make signs for the school trash cans that say, "Put Litter Here."

❍ Invite the children to add another verse to the song. For example, "Let's clean up all the trash…," "Let's take care of each other…," or "Let's recycle and reuse…." Print the new verse on chart paper as the children dictate the words they want to use.

✔ **English Language Learner Strategy:** Next to some of the words in the new verse, place pictures of the words so the child will more easily understand their meaning.

Oral Language/Print Awareness

❍ Make a list of ways to keep the Earth clean. *How can we keep the land areas of the earth clean? How can we keep the water areas clean?*

✔ **Special Needs Adaptation:** Keep in mind that children with special needs—especially those with autism and cognitive challenges—often have trouble with abstract concepts. They may have difficulty understanding the difference between "cleaning an object," such as a car, and "cleaning the Earth." Use pictures to demonstrate the difference.

Curriculum Connections

Art

❍ Provide clean, recyclable, trash items, such as bottle caps, empty toilet paper tubes, cardboard meat trays, and so on. Provide glue and challenge the children to use the trash to build a sculpture.

○ Invite the children to draw pictures showing people and animals sharing the Earth.

Construction

○ Provide small lunch sacks and crayons. Encourage the children to decorate the bags to create car litter bags.

Discovery

○ Provide pictures of animals that are on the endangered species list. Discuss the animals and what caused them to become endangered. Information about endangered species can be found on the following website—http://endangered.fws.gov/wildlife.html.

Field Trip

○ Take a field trip to the zoo. Find animals in the zoo that are on the endangered species list. Discuss things that can be done to help preserve the animals.

Gross Motor

○ Use masking tape to make a throw line on the floor. Give the children wadded-up paper (use paper that can be recycled) to use as balls and a trash can to toss the paper into. When the children have finished, count the number of pieces of litter (missed shots) on the floor. Discuss what would happen if the paper wasn't picked up and recycled.

Outdoors

○ Provide trash bags and plastic gloves and encourage the children to pick up litter on the playground.

Science

○ Provide pictures of animals and their homes. Invite the children to match the animals to their home.

Home Activities

○ Suggest that families make it a habit to work together to pick up trash that blows into their yard.
○ Suggest that families help their children make "Do Not Litter" signs for their car.

White Coral Bells

White coral bells
Upon a slender stalk,
Lilies of the valley
Deck my garden walk.
Oh, don't you wish
That you could hear them ring?
That will happen only
When the fairies sing.

Vocabulary

coral bell
deck
fairy
garden
lily
ring
slender
stalk
valley
walk

Did You Know?

○ The "white coral bells" in this song are Lilies of the Valley, which are beautiful white flowers. The flowers are shaped like tiny bells, which is where they get their name, and hang down the stem in a long row, hidden between dark green oval leaves.

○ Lilies of the Valley have clusters of small, white, bell-shaped flowers that hang from a strong reedy stalk. There may be a dozen or more blossoms per plant. Their outstanding feature is their sweet fragrance, which has inspired perfumes. The best way to appreciate the fragrance is to plant Lilies of the Valley along a walkway or in raised containers that you pass by regularly.

○ This is a traditional campfire song and is often sung in rounds. It is popular with Girl Scouts throughout North America and around the world.

Theme Connections

Colors
Flowers
Growing Things

Literacy Links

Oral Language

○ Define words that may be new vocabulary for the children; for example, *coral bells*, *slender*, *stalk*, *lilies*, and *deck*.

✓ **English Language Learner Strategy:** Provide pictures of the words so the children will more easily understand the meaning of the words.

Phonological Awareness/Print Awareness
❍ Print the song on chart paper. Read it to the children. Read it a second time, stopping as you come to the second rhyming word in a rhyming word pair; for example, *walk* and *sing*. Let the children fill in the word. Underline it when they say it. Discuss rhyming words. Point out how the rhyming pattern helps us remember the words of the song.

Curriculum Connections

Art
❍ Invite the children to paint white flowers.

Circle Time
❍ Provide bells for the children to ring while they sing. You can use hand bells if they are available. If not available, make your own bells by placing jingle bells inside envelopes and sealing them.

Discovery
❍ Provide a variety of seeds for the children to examine. Provide a magnifying glass so smaller seeds can be seen more clearly. Provide tweezers for the children to use when trying to hold or move the smaller seeds. *Which seeds roll easily? Which seeds are difficult to roll? What makes the difference? Can you see the shape of the seeds better when looking through the magnifying glass? Which seeds can be moved easily by blowing on them?*

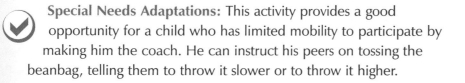

Gross Motor
❍ Provide a service bell and a beanbag. Prepare a throw line by placing a strip of masking tape on the floor. Challenge the children to ring the bell. Have them sing when they toss. Does it help them ring the bell?

✔ **Special Needs Adaptations:** This activity provides a good opportunity for a child who has limited mobility to participate by making him the coach. He can instruct his peers on tossing the beanbag, telling them to throw it slower or to throw it higher.

Book Corner

Flower Garden by
   Eve Bunting
From Seed to Plant
   by Gail Gibbons
Planting a Rainbow
   by Lois Elhert
Sunflower House by
   Eve Bunting
The Tiny Seed by Eric
   Carle

Math

○ Cut a wide slit and a slender slit in the top of a box. Provide wide and slender items, such as craft sticks, rulers, pencils, crayons, straws, and plastic knives. Challenge the children to experiment with the items to determine whether they are slender or wide as defined by the slits in the box.

Music

○ Collect empty tin cans of various sizes. Cover the open ends of cans with duct tape to protect children from the cut edges. Turn five or six cans over and arrange them by size, from smallest to largest. Provide a pencil, drumstick, or dowel and invite the children to ring these "bells" by tapping on them with their sticks. *How does the sound of the smallest can differ from the sound of the largest can? What happens to the sound when you hit the cans from smallest to largest?*

Music and Movement

○ Talk about fairies. *What do they do? How do they move? Where do they live?* Play classical music and invite the children to dance like fairies flitting through a garden.

Outdoors

○ Prepare and plant a small garden or flower bed. If garden space is limited, use a large barrel or a planter box. Discuss the importance of making sure there is good drainage and using the right soil. Allow the children to plant the seeds and oversee the care of the garden.

Home Activity

○ Ask the children to find out the name of one of the flowers that are growing at or near their homes.

Twinkle, Twinkle, Little Star

Vocabulary

blazing	blue
curtain	dark
dew	diamond
peep	set
shut	star
sun	twinkle
wet	wonder

Theme Connections

Day and Night
Nature

Twinkle, twinkle, little star,
How I wonder what you are!
Up above the world so high,
Like a diamond in the sky,
Twinkle, twinkle little star
How I wonder what you are!

When the blazing sun is set,
And the grass with dew is wet,
Then you show your little light.
Twinkle, twinkle all the night,
Twinkle, twinkle little star,
How I wonder what you are!

In the dark blue sky you keep,
Often through my curtains peep.
For you never shut your eye
'Til the sun is in the sky,
Twinkle, twinkle little star,
How I wonder what you are!

Did You Know?

○ "Twinkle, Twinkle Little Star" is a traditional nursery rhyme, written by two sisters, Ann Taylor (1782-1866) and Jane Taylor (1783-1824). The rhyme was published in 1806.

○ Stars seen from outer space do not twinkle; it is only when viewed from Earth that they appear to twinkle. Tiny irregularities in the density, humidity, and temperature of the air drift in front of stars as we view them through the atmosphere. When a beam of starlight travels through the atmosphere, these irregularities disturb the beam, causing it to "dance" back and forth, or to "twinkle."

Literacy Links

Oral Language

○ Sing the first verse of the song using different adjectives to describe the star; for example, gigantic, enormous, jazzy, and silent. Change your voice to match the adjective. For example, if you sing about a tiny star, sing it with a tiny voice. If you sing about a jazzy star, sing the song with a jazzy beat.

○ Teach the children the American Sign Language sign for *star* (page 121).
○ Teach the children the rhyme "Star Light, Star Bright."

Star Light, Star Bright
Star light, star bright,
The brightest star I see tonight.
I wish I may, I wish I might,
Have this wish I wish tonight.

Encourage each child to make a wish and to share it aloud.

Phonological Awareness/Letter Knowledge
○ Print *star* on chart paper. Challenge the children to think of words that rhyme with *star*. Write the rhyming words on the chart paper. Ask the children to determine how each rhyming word is different from *star* and how each word is like *star*.

 English Language Learner Strategy: Provide pictures of words that rhyme with star.

Curriculum Connections

Art
○ Cut blue bulletin board paper to fit an easel. Place the paper on an easel with white tempera paint. Add silver glitter to the paint. Invite the children to create a starry night picture.

Cooking
○ Place a popcorn popper in the center of the floor on top of a vinyl tablecloth. Pop the corn without the lid on the popper so the corn pops out of the popper like shooting stars. When the popcorn is finished popping and is cool enough to eat, invite the children to eat the "stars" (popcorn) right off the tablecloth.

Discovery
○ Provide a flashlight and a plastic bottle of water. Invite the children to shake the water and then shine the flashlight through the water and onto the wall. *Does the light twinkle?*

Field Trip
○ Take the children to a planetarium.

Fine Motor

○ Provide cardboard stars to use as templates. Encourage the children to trace the templates onto drawing paper to create a sky full of stars.

Language

○ Cut large stars from drawing paper. Invite the children to draw a picture of something they would wish for if they were wishing on a star.

Math

○ Create counting mats by printing numerals on sheets of blue construction paper. Provide tweezers and cups of rock salt to symbolize stars. Encourage the children to use the tweezers to move the appropriate number of "stars" (pieces of rock salt) from the container onto counting mats.

 Special Needs Adaptation: For children with physical limitations, adapt the activity by placing a mat of another color (yellow or green) next to the child's blue construction paper counting mat. Pour rock salt onto the other mat and encourage the child to move the rock salt to her counting mat using a tongue depressor or a paintbrush rather than tweezers. The tongue depressor and the paintbrush are easier to hold and the child can still fully participate in the activity.

Outdoors

○ Invite the children to play Star Catch. Draw stars on beanbags or tape stars to the beanbags. Give the children a bucket (an empty half-gallon ice cream container works well). Challenge them to catch a beanbag in their "bucket" when you toss the beanbags into the air.

Home Activity

○ Encourage families to star gaze with their children.

Book Corner

Goodnight, Moon by Margaret Wise Brown
Hush, Little Baby by Sylvia Long
Sleepytime Rhyme by Remy Charlip
Twinkle, Twinkle, Little Star by Sylvia Long (illustrator)
Twinkle, Twinkle, Little Star by Iza Trapani (illustrator)

SONGS AND ACTIVITIES

Mister Sun

Oh, Mister Sun, Sun, Mister Golden Sun,
Won't you please shine down on me?
Oh, Mister Sun, Sun, Mister Golden Sun,
Hiding behind that tree.
These little children are asking you
To please come out
So they can play with you.
Oh, Mister Sun, Sun, Mister Golden Sun,
Won't you please shine down on,
Talk about your shine on,
Please shine down on me!

Vocabulary

down
golden
hiding
little
Mister
shine

Theme Connections

Day and Night
Nature

Did You Know?

○ The sun is a star, a bright star! It is the largest star in our solar system, and it is the center of our solar system.

○ The sun is white, like other hot stars. It appears yellow to us against the blue background of the sky.

○ Never look at the sun without eye protection. Looking at it without protection can cause blindness.

○ We think of the Earth as a big place. The sun is almost 100 times wider than the Earth. It is like placing a marble next to a basketball.

○ The sun makes life on our planet possible by providing great amounts of light and heat. The Earth has no light of its own. Without the sun, the Earth would be dark.

Literacy Links

Comprehension

○ Discuss the use of the title, *Mister*. Ask the children why they think the songwriter chose to say Mister Sun instead of Mrs. Sun. Sing the song using Mrs. Sun instead of Mister Sun.

Oral Language

○ Show the children a picture of a sunny scene. Discuss what is seen in the picture. Talk about activities that are good to do on a sunny day.

○ Teach the children the American Sign Language sign for *sun* (page 121).

○ Share the listening story, "The Wind and the Sun" (page 106) with the children. Encourage them to create their own illustrations for the story by using their imagination.

(✓) **English Language Learner Strategy:** Provide pictures of words in the story so the children will more easily understand the meaning of the story.

Oral Language/Print Awareness

○ Discuss sun safety; for example, wearing sunglasses, not looking directly at the sun, and using sunscreen. Help the children make a list of Sun Safety Rules. Invite them to illustrate the rules and display the rules in the classroom.

(✓) **Special Needs Adaptation:** Adapt this activity to include outside safety rules, as well. The importance of safety is critical for children with special needs. They may not understand basic rules; for example, staying away from outside water sources, not leaving a play area or yard without asking an adult, not chasing a ball into the street, and so on. Tell them that all outside water is off-limits unless an adult is present. Mention that outside water, including rainwater, is not safe to drink. When talking about sun safety, stress that sunscreen should be applied only when an adult is present.

Curriculum Connections

Art

○ On a sunny day, give each child a sheet of blue or black construction paper. Have the children take their paper outdoors and lay it in the sun. Encourage them to collect outdoor items such as leaves, sticks, and rocks, and place those items in a design of their choice on their paper. Leave the papers in the sun for a few hours. When the children return and remove the items from their paper, they will see that the design remains on the paper. Explain that the heat of the sun can drain the color from a colored item when it is not covered. The sun has bleached the color from those places on the papers that were not covered by leaves, rocks, and sticks.

Discovery

❍ Place a prism in a sunny window and watch the patterns created by the sun's position.

❍ Help the children make decaffeinated Sun Tea. Place decaffeinated tea bags in a pitcher of water and place the pitcher in the sun for a couple of hours. The sun will warm the water and brew the tea.

 English Language Learner Strategy: Create a rebus for this recipe to make it easier for the child to follow the directions.

Games

❍ Go outside and play a game of Shadow Tag. To play Shadow Tag, each child must first find a partner. One of the pair is designated as IT. IT chases the other child and attempts to step on or tag the other child's shadow. When IT is successful, the partners change roles and the game begins again. Ask the children how the sun is participating in the game. Are they playing with the sun as the song suggests?

Language

❍ Make Sun Puzzles. Cut round circles from yellow poster board to represent suns. Draw a happy face on the suns. Cut each sun into puzzle pieces. Encourage the children to put the puzzles together.

Math

❍ Demonstrate the difference in size between the sun and the Earth by placing 100 marbles in a straight line and then placing 1 marble next to the line of 100. Explain that the Earth is the width of one marble and the sun is the width of 100 marbles. *Why does the sun seem smaller than the Earth?*

Outdoors

❍ Take the children outdoors on a sunny day and explore the shadows they make with their bodies. Have them stand with their backs to the sun and then find their own shadow. Show them how to make their shadows grow larger and smaller. Encourage them to squat, jump, and make funny shadow shapes.

Science

○ Use a stick or powdered paint to draw a circle 6' in diameter in a sunny spot on the playground. Place a 6' dowel in the ground in the center of the circle. Early in the morning, place a block on the place where the shadow of the dowel crosses the perimeter of the circle. At noon, the shadow should have moved to the same position as the hands on a clock, or north. Place a block at this location. If the children are interested, you can continue to place blocks around the perimeter each hour. Some children will notice how the rotation matches the clock, while others will just be excited to see how the shadows made by the sun change over time.

Home Activity

○ Encourage the children to discuss their favorite sunny day activities with their families.

Rain, Rain, Go Away

(additional verses by Pam Schiller)

Rain, rain, go away.
Little children want to play.

Clouds, clouds, go away.
Little children want to play.

Thunder, thunder, go away.
Little children want to play.

Rain, rain, come back soon.
Little flowers want to bloom.

✓ **English Language Learner Strategy:** Recite the verses of the song before singing it, so children can hear the words and experience the rhythms of the song lyrics.

bloom
cloud
come back
flower
go away
little
play
rain
thunder

Theme Connections

Nature
Weather

Did You Know?

○ We will never have any more water in our world than we do at this moment. The water in our lakes, rivers, oceans, seas, and even our swimming pools is constantly "evaporating"—rising up to the sky.
We cannot see water when it evaporates. When it goes into the sky, evaporated water makes clouds. The clouds move with the breeze, and may move over another part of Earth. When the clouds finally are so full of water they need to let some of it go, they release the water in the form of rain, snow, hail, or sleet.

○ When rain hits the ground, some of it soaks into the dirt and some goes back into the rivers, lakes, oceans, seas, and even our swimming pools. This cycle is ongoing as the air and ground clean the water and recycle it.

○ Louisiana is the wettest state in the United States.

○ Cherrapunji, India receives more rain than any other place in the world.

○ It rains 350 days a year on Mt. Waialeale in Kauai, Hawaii.

Literacy Links

Phonological Awareness

○ Discuss the sounds rain makes as it falls to the ground; for example, splish, splash; drip, drop; pitter, and patter. These sounds are called *onomatopoeia*—words that sound like the sound they are describing. Ask the children to think of *onomatopoeic* words that describe thunder.

Print Awareness

○ Print the first verse of the song on chart paper. Point to the words as the children sing the song.

Oral Language/Print Awareness

○ Discuss rainy days. Ask the children what they like to do on a rainy day and write their ideas on a sheet of chart paper.

Curriculum Connections

Art

○ Invite the children to draw a picture of something they enjoy doing on a rainy day.

Special Needs Adaptation: Cut out pictures of rainy day activities from newspapers or a magazine and encourage the child to make a Rainy Day Picture Collection by gluing the photos onto drawing paper. If he has difficulty applying the glue, pour glue onto a paper plate and give him a paintbrush to use to apply the glue. Encourage peer participation by making a class mural of things to do on a rainy day. The mural can be a combination of drawn pictures and pictures the children find in magazines.

Dramatic Play

○ Place rain gear, such as boots, hats, raincoats, and ponchos, in the center for children to discover and try on.

Gross Motor

○ Cut large white cloud shapes from white butcher paper. Place the "clouds" on the floor. Invite the children to pretend to be airplanes and fly through the clouds.

Special Needs Adaptation: For children with limited mobility, provide wadded-up paper balls and encourage them to toss their paper balls onto a cloud.

Book Corner

The Cloud Book by Tomie dePaola
Flash, Crash, Rumble, and Roll by Franklyn M. Branley
Listen to the Rain by Bill Martin, Jr.
Rain by Robert Kalan
Thunder Cake by Patricia Polacco

Listening

❍ Provide a spray bottle of water and a variety of surfaces to spray it on, such as a cookie sheet, a plastic place mat, a wooden bowl, a sheet of paper, or other surfaces. Encourage the children to experiment by spraying water on different surfaces. *How does the surface affect the sound of the water hitting it?*

Math

❍ Collect rainwater in a shallow tub. Measure how much rain falls. Use rainwater for classroom activities—to water plants, to make watercolor paints, or as bath water for baby dolls.

Music

❍ Provide drums, spray bottles filled with water, and surfaces to spray. Challenge the children to combine the sounds of the drums and the sound of the water from the spray bottles to create a rainstorm. Have the children start the storm slowly, build to a crescendo, and then slowly end the storm. *Do the rain and the wind make music?*

Music and Movement

❍ Play classical music and invite the children to dance like raindrops, then like a rainstorm, and finally like a quiet gentle rain.

Outdoors

❍ Put the top of a trash can or a large shallow tub outside to make a birdbath. Let it fill with rainwater. Encourage the children to watch the birds bathe, frolic in, and drink from their birdbath.

Science

❍ Fill a glass half full of water and cover it tightly with plastic wrap, using a rubber band to secure it. Place the glass of water in the refrigerator for two hours. When you take it out, you will see that there are water droplets on the inside of the glass on the plastic. The longer you wait, the more droplets will form. Place the glass on a table. When the glass warms, the water in the droplets will begin to fall from the plastic back into the glass. You have made rain!

Home Activity

❍ Suggest that the children talk with their families about their favorite rainy day activities.

We've Got the Whole World in Our Hands

Vocabulary

recycle
reduce
reuse
take care
whole
world

Theme Connections

Conservation
Environment
Recycling

Did You Know?

O Recycling means using something more than once. Lots of the things can be recycled, such as newspapers, glass, aluminum, and many plastic items.

O Reusing things means we don't have to make as many new things. This saves money, energy, and resources.

O Reducing our use of resources is called *conservation*. We must work *with* nature, using only our fair share of resources and recognizing that every action we take affects the Earth.

O The Earth constantly recycles air and water. When we take a bath or shower, the water goes into sewers, is purified and returned to lakes and rivers, where it then evaporates, forms clouds and rains down on the

adapted by Pam Schiller

(Tune: He's Got the Whole World in His Hands)
We've got the whole world in our hands.
We've got the whole wide world in our hands.
We've got the whole world in our hands.
We've got the whole world in our hands.

Let's reduce all our trash…And take care of our world.
Reduce all our trash…And take care of our world.
Reduce all our trash…And take care of our world.
We've got the whole world in our hands.

Let's reuse all we can… And take care of our world.
Reuse all we can… And take care of our world.
Reuse all we can… And take care of our world.
We've got the whole world in our hands.

Let's recycle all we can… And take care of our world.
Recycle all we can… And take care of our world.
Recycle all we can… And take care of our world.
We've got the whole world in our hands.

Reduce, reuse, recycle…Takin' care of our world.
Reduce, reuse, recycle…Takin' care of our world.
Reduce, reuse, recycle…Takin' care of our world.
We've got the whole world in our hands. Yeah!

Earth. Then it is collected in lakes, rivers, and reservoirs, is purified and is piped into our homes. The cycle then starts again.

○ April 22 is Earth Day, an international day of celebration when we can show our respect for the Earth.

Literacy Links

Letter Knowledge

○ Print *reuse*, *reduce*, and *recycle* on chart paper. Discuss each word. Ask the children to identify the first two letters in each word. Recite the words, stressing the first two letters.

Oral Language

○ Discuss recycling clothing that the children have outgrown.

Print Awareness

○ Show the children an empty toilet paper tube. Ask them to think of uses for the tubes. Make a list of their ideas.

○ Help the children make a list of things that can be reused, such as ribbons and bows, containers, clothing, scraps of paper, and scraps of fabric.

> **✓ Special Needs Adaptation:** Display reuseable items. Describe each item and how it was originally used. Suggest ways the items can be reused. Make sure the child understands the meaning of *reuse*. Be specific. *Reuse* means to use again or use over and over. Encourage the child to point to things in the classroom that are reused.

Segmentation

○ Have the children clap the syllables in *reuse*, *reduce*, and *recycle*. Ask the children to stand up and shake their hips to the syllables in the phrase.

Curriculum Connections

Art

○ Provide scraps of paper, fabric, bows, and other materials. Encourage the children to make a collage with the scraps.

Blocks

○ Fill the block center with empty toilet paper and paper towel tubes, cardboard boxes, and paper bags. Encourage the children to find ways to use the items in their building with blocks.

Dramatic Play

○ Provide a variety of clothing in a variety of sizes. Encourage the children to find items that are too small for them.

Language

○ Show the children the symbol for recycling. Provide a variety of items for the children to sort according to whether they can be recycled.

Music

○ Make kazoos. Provide empty toilet paper tubes for each child. Encourage each child to decorate a tube. Cover the end of the tube with wax paper and secure with a rubber band. Show the children how to blow through the open end of the toilet paper tube to create music.

Outdoors

○ Encourage the children to pick up trash on the playground and around the school.

Science

○ Melt small bits of crayons to make new crayons. Sort the crayons into empty cans by color. With adult supervision, help the children place the cans into a cold electric skillet. Put the skillet out of the reach of the children and set on a low temperature. When the crayons melt, pour each color into a separate space of a muffin tin (adults only). Let the crayons cool out of the reach of the children. Discuss the value of recycling the crayons. **Safety note:** Closely supervise the children during this activity.

The Great Kapok Tree: A Tale of the Amazon Rain Forest by Lynne Cherry

The Hunt for Spring by Susan O'Halloran

The Lorax by Dr. Seuss

Recycle!: A Handbook for Kids by Gail Gibbons

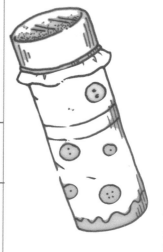

Home Activities

○ Ask families to provide junk materials, such as bottle caps, buttons, and old keys, for sorting boxes.

○ Ask families to save recyclable items for classroom projects, such as egg cartons, meat trays, orange juice cans, and empty thread spools.

○ Suggest that families involve their children in garage sales and collection of items for Goodwill Industries or similar agencies. Encourage them to discuss reusing items as they participate in these activities.

○ Suggest that families organize recycling bins.

SONGS AND ACTIVITIES

Under the Spreading Chestnut Tree

Under the spreading chestnut tree, *(cup hands together as if digging under something, then bring elbows together and hold arms up and spread fingers to make a tree, then touch your chest, then your head, and then fan fingers like a tree)*
There I held her on my knee. *(slap knees)*
We were happy, yesiree, *(jog in place as if happy)*
Under the spreading chestnut tree! *(bring elbows together and hold arms up and spread fingers to make a tree, tap chest, and then head; then fan fingers to make a tree)*
(Repeat)

✓ **Special Needs Adaptation:** Modeling and practice are important tools in teaching new concepts to children with special needs. Model each step of the hand and body movements for the song. Show one movement, such as cupping hands for digging, and then ask the child to do that movement with you several times before learning the next movement. Explaining new concepts in simple steps or asking a child to do only one movement is easier than learning the steps all at once.

Vocabulary

chestnut
knee
spreading
yesiree

Theme Connections

Food/Nutrition
Growing Things
Nature

Did You Know?

- ❍ The chestnut tree was once the dominant species over most of the forests in the Eastern United States. The chestnut tree was destroyed by a fungus that was accidentally imported and to which the trees had no resistance.
- ❍ Before the chestnut tree was destroyed, it played a big part in the lives of the people and animals on the East Coast. Wildlife of many kinds depended on its nuts, which fell in abundance. People depended on the nuts, too, as did their livestock. They were not only tasty, but also nutritious.
- ❍ The chestnut tree provided timber unrivaled in quality. Straight-grained and strong, easy to work with and rot-resistant, chestnut lumber went into barn beams and furniture, as well as many other items.
- ❍ Chestnuts have a sweet, nutty flavor. The texture is like a firm baked potato, quite unlike other nuts, which are crunchy.
- ❍ Chestnuts are a favorite winter snack. Perhaps the line from "The Christmas Song," "chestnuts roasting on an open fire" adds to the popularity of chestnuts during the holidays.

Literacy Links

Oral Language

○ Sing the song substituting the names of other trees, such as white oak, maple, and willow. *Does changing the name of the tree change the meaning of the song?*

○ Discuss the hand motions that go with the song. Explain that hands can be used to communicate. Sing the song twice. Sing the lyrics and do the hand motions the first time you sing it. The second time, just hum the song and do the hand motions. *Can you figure out what the song is about by watching the hand motions, without hearing the lyrics?*

○ Share the following poem "Shade Tree" with the children. Ask them to sequence the Seed-to-Fruit sequence cards (page 107).

Shade Tree
Seed turns to plant and plant into tree
With mighty branches just to hold
Leaves, fruit, and me.

Oral Language/Print Awareness

○ Make a Word Web (page 118). Print *trees* in the center of a sheet of chart paper. Draw a circle around the word. Ask the children to tell you what they know about trees. Discuss the many uses; for example, enjoying the fruit, enjoying the shade, building with the wood, using the branches for hanging swings, and for holding tree houses. Discuss the care trees need. Write the things the children say on lines that extend out from the circle. Add to the Word Web as you learn new things about trees.

✓ **English Language Learner Strategy:** Provide pictures of the words in the Word Web so the child will more easily understand the meaning of the words.

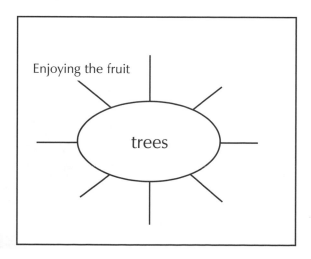

Curriculum Connections

Art

○ Provide glue, paper, brown paper for trunks and branches, and green tempera paint and sponges to make leaves. Ask the children to cut or tear trunks and branches from the brown paper and glue them to their papers. Show them how to use a sponge and the green paint to make leaves on their tree. Provide a brown marker to make chestnuts in the trees. If you create a large tree, you may want to cut the sponges into leaf shapes. When viewed from a distance, sponges will create the visual effect of leaves.

○ Make hand trees. Provide brown and green fingerpaint. Paint one of each child's hands with brown paint and encourage the children to spread their fingers and press their hand onto their drawing paper. Point out that the results look like a tree trunk and branches. Have the children wash their hands, and then press their fingertips into the green paint to make fingerprint leaves on the branches of their tree.

Fine Motor

○ Use masking tape to make two parallel lines, 6" apart, on a tabletop. Provide chestnuts for the children to roll. Since the nuts are not completely round, this is more difficult than it sounds. Have the children use only their index fingers to gently tap the nuts through the lines. The object is to get the nut to the end of the table without it rolling outside the lines.

Gross Motor

○ Give each child a chestnut. Have the children stand on one foot with their other foot up as if marching. Challenge them to place a chestnut on their knee and balance it while counting to five. Have them try again, this time balancing the chestnut on the top of their raised foot.

✔ **Special Needs Adaptation:** Encourage children with limited mobility to balance the chestnut on the back of their hand.

Language

○ Print *chestnut* on five separate 4" x 6" strips of poster board, leaving a small space between the "t" at the end of *chest* and the "n" at the beginning of *nut*. Cut the words *chest* and *nut* apart with puzzle cuts. Give the children all ten pieces of poster board (five that say *chest* and five that say *nut*) and invite them to find the two pieces that go together to make up the word chestnut. Discuss that the word *chestnut* can be divided into two words. Explain that when two words that could stand alone are combined they are called *compound words*.

Science

○ Give the children the Seed-to-Fruit sequence cards (page 107). Encourage them to sequence the cards from seed to tree to fruit.

Snack

○ Provide chestnuts for snack. Show the children how to crack the shell and free the meat from the nut.

Home Activity

○ Suggest that families plant small trees in their yards and enjoy watching them grow with their children.

Little Drop of Dew

Little drop of dew, of dew
Like a gem you are.
I believe that you
Must have been a star.

When the day is light, is light
On the grass you lie.
Tell me then at night
Are you in the sky?
(Repeat)

Vocabulary

dew
gem
grass
light
night
sky
star

Theme Connections

Nature
Seasons

Did You Know?

❍ For dew to form, the ideal conditions are high humidity near the ground, low humidity in the air above, little or no wind, and a cloud-free sky. The lack of cloud cover allows the ground to radiate heat upwards; the heat then cools, allowing condensation to occur. The warm, moist air close to the ground allows dew to form.

❍ Dew gives everything a light cover of moisture, making it look as if a light rain has fallen.

❍ If the layer of low, moist air is thicker, dew and even fog will occur. Water droplets will merge more readily on the ground, as solid areas are an ideal surface for condensation to take place. Dew can occur without fog, but fog cannot occur without dew.

❍ "Little Drop of Dew" is a popular camp song.

Literacy Links

Oral Language

❍ Define words in the song that the children may not be familiar with, such as *dew* and *gem*. Some children may not have ever seen dew, or if they have, they may have thought it was rain if no one told them otherwise. Show the children various gems, and point out how shiny the stones are. Look at the gems under a light. Ask the children why the songwriter compares dew to gems.

✓ **Special Needs Adaptation:** Instead of asking the child why the songwriter compares dew to gems, explain the concept of comparing things in everyday life. Many children with special needs can compare items but they are not aware that comparing is what they are doing. Teach the concept of comparing, and practice it throughout the day. Start by teaching simple comparisons, such as *big* and *little*, *tall* and *short*, and so on.

Phonological Awareness

○ Print the song on chart paper and underline the rhyming words. Have the children repeat the pairs of rhyming words so they are able to hear the likenesses in the words. Sing the song again and pause before the second rhyming word, allowing the children to say the second word in a rhyming word pair. See how many words you can rhyme with dew. There are quite a few!

Print Awareness

○ Print the song on chart paper and point to each word as the children sing the song. This song is slow enough and short enough to allow this to be a valuable activity to demonstrate the left-to-right and top-to-bottom direction of print. Call attention to the space between the words.

Curriculum Connections

Art

○ Invite the children to paint a picture using sparkly paint. Mix ½ cup salt with 1 pint tempera paint. Use immediately, before the salt breaks down. Suggest that the children paint a picture of their house and then use the sparkly paint to paint the ground around their home to simulate dew-covered grass.

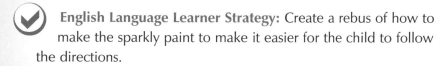

✓ **English Language Learner Strategy:** Create a rebus of how to make the sparkly paint to make it easier for the child to follow the directions.

Discovery

○ Provide spray bottles filled with water, scraps of fabric and paper, paper towels, and a cookie sheet. Set the spray bottles to spray a fine mist. Encourage the children to spray their water bottles over the various items you have supplied. *Which items soak up the moisture? Which items repel the moisture?*

Special Needs Adaptation: Encourage the children to work with a peer buddy. Have one child spray the items and the other determine which items soaked up the moisture.

Fine Motor

○ Mix grass and rock salt together in a small tub. Provide tweezers for the children to use to remove the salt (dew) from the grass.

Math

○ Provide a box of stones—some shiny and some dull—and a flashlight or other light source. Encourage the children to look at the stones with the light shining on them and then to sort them into two categories—stones that are shiny and stones that are not shiny.

Outdoors

○ It takes seven or more players to play this game. Divide the players into two groups: Stars and Catchers. Set up two boundaries about 20' apart. Catchers stand in the middle of the two boundaries. Stars stand on one side of the boundaries. Catchers say, "Star light, star bright, how many stars are out tonight?" Stars say, "More than you can catch!" The stars run across to the other end, trying not to get tagged. Stars who are tagged become catchers until everyone is a catcher and there are no stars left.

○ Give the children an eyedropper and water. Invite them to drop "dewdrops" (water) onto the grass. *What do the drops look like? Do they look like dew on the grass? Can they drop a drop of water on a single blade of grass? Does the water roll down the blade of grass?*

Science

○ Use an eyedropper to place several drops of water on the bottom of a glass pie dish. Place the dish on a rack that allows children to look at the water from the bottom of the dish. Provide a flashlight and invite the children to use it to look at the water drops from under the dish. Have them shine a light on the water drops from the top. Provide a magnifying glass to take a closer look. *What does the drop look like up close? Does it look different with a flashlight shining on it? Does is look different when looking at it from under the dish than it does when looking at it from above the dish?*

Book Corner

Writing

○ Use markers to print *dew* on coffee filters. Provide eyedroppers and blue water (add a few drops of blue food coloring to water). Encourage the children to use an eyedropper to drop "dewdrops" (water) over the letters.

Home Activity

○ Suggest that families take their children outside early in the morning to see the dew. *Does the dew "twinkle" like stars?*

The Weather Song

(Tune: Clementine)
Sunny, sunny,
Sunny, sunny,
It is sunny in the sky.
S-u-n-n-y, sunny,
It is sunny in the sky.

Cloudy, cloudy,
Cloudy, cloudy,
It is cloudy in the sky.
C-l-o-u-d-y, cloudy
It is cloudy in the sky.

Snowy, snowy,
Snowy, snowy,
It is snowy in the sky.
S-n-o-w-y, snowy,
It is snowy in the sky.

Foggy, foggy,
Foggy, foggy,
It is foggy in the sky.
F-o-g-g-y, foggy,
It is foggy in the sky.

Vocabulary

foggy
rainy
sky
snowy
sunny

Theme Connections

Seasons
Weather

Did You Know?

○ Weather reports are provided every day in the newspaper, on the radio, and on television.
○ See page 50 for weather facts.

Literacy Links

Oral Language

○ Teach the children the fingerplay, "April Clouds."

April Clouds
Two little clouds one April day (hold both hands in fists)
Went sailing across the sky. (move fists toward each other)
They went so fast, they bumped their heads, (bump fists together)
And both began to cry. (point to eyes)

The big round sun came out and said, (make circle with arms)
"Oh, never mind, my dears,
*   I'll send all my sunbeams down* (wiggle fingers downward like rain)
*   like rain)*
*   To dry your fallen tears."*

English Language Learner Strategy: Model the actions for the children until they are able to follow along without assistance from you.

Print Awareness

o Use "The Weather Song" rebus cards (page 117) to represent every type of weather mentioned in the song. Print one verse of the song, leaving a blank space where the weather type is mentioned. Place the rebus pictures where they belong for each verse. Have the children sing the song while you point to the words.

Segmentation

o Clap the letters in each weather word—*sunny, cloudy, rainy,* and *foggy.* Clap the syllables in each word. *Are there more letters or syllables in each word?*

 Special Needs Adaptation: Encourage children with motor challenges to use alternative means of clapping; for example, beating a drum or tapping a service bell.

Letter Knowledge/Phonological Awareness

o Print *sunny, rainy,* and *foggy* on a sheet of chart paper. Have the children count the letters in each word. Have them look at the words. *Which letter is in all three words? Where does that letter appear in each word?* Say the words. *Can you hear a similar sound at the end of each word?*

Curriculum Connections

Art

o Provide orange and yellow paints. Suggest that the children paint suns.

Dramatic Play

o Provide clothing appropriate for many kinds of weather. Encourage the children to sort the clothing and to explore dressing for different types of weather. Provide a mirror.

Fine Motor

○ Make Cloud Dough. Mix 1 cup vegetable oil, 6 cups flour, and 1 cup water. Add additional water if necessary, 1 tablespoon at a time—just enough to bind the mixture. Encourage the children to shape clouds with their dough.

 English Language Learner Strategy: Use a rebus (page 114) for this recipe to make it easier for the child to follow directions for making Cloud Dough.

Gross Motor

○ Twirl a prism in a sunny window to create moving rainbows Challenge the children to step on a rainbow.

○ Cut raindrops the size of quarters from blue construction paper and attach one end of each to a 12" piece of yarn to each raindrop. Attach the second end of the yarn to the underside of a table. Challenge the children to crawl under the table from one end to the other without disturbing any of the raindrops, in other words, without getting wet!

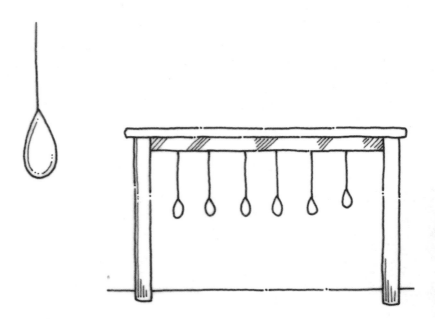

Language

○ Give the children "The Weather Song" rebus cards and encourage them to use the cards to sing the song.

Listening

○ Encourage the children to create the sounds of a thunderstorm by beating on a drum and spraying spray bottles of water rapidly onto a sheet of plastic.

Music and Movement

❍ Give the children blue crepe paper streamers to represent "rain" and have them dance to classical music that has a variety of tempos. Encourage them to dance like a soft rain. Encourage them to dance like a thunderstorm.

✓ **Special Needs Adaptation:** For children with limited mobility, give them drums and encourage them to provide the sounds of thunder. Provide pompoms, like those used by cheerleaders, to create the swooshing sound of the wind.

Writing

❍ Print the words that describe each type of weather on chart paper. Provide magnetic letters and invite the children to copy the words.

The Cloud Book by Tomie de Paola
Flash, Crash, Rumble, and Roll by Franklin M. Branley
Foggy Friday by Phyllis Root
Weather: Poems for All Seasons by Lee Bennett Hopkins

Home Activity

❍ Encourage families to discuss weather with their children. Suggest that they introduce their child to the weather maps in the newspaper, or to the weather channel on TV.

It's Raining

with additional verse by Richele Bartkowiak

It's raining, it's pouring
The old man is snoring.
He bumped his head
When he went to bed,
And he couldn't get up in the morning.

It's raining, it's pouring
Playing inside is boring.
We want sunshine
And bright blue skies.
Don't make us wait till morning.

Vocabulary

blue
bright
bump
inside
morning
pouring
snoring
sunshine
wait

Theme Connections

Humor
Nature
Seasons
Weather

Did You Know?

○ Snoring is noisy breathing through the mouth or nose during sleep. Most people snore every so often. People snore when they are congested. Even babies or pets snore.

○ Sleep and relaxation go hand-in-hand. During deep sleep, the muscles in the body relax; as the muscles in the throat relax, the airway closes partly. This is normal. Air comes into and out of the lungs through this airway. However, if the airflow in the throat and nose is obstructed, the air passage narrows, and snoring is the result. Snoring is the fluttering sound created by the vibrations of tissues in the back of the throat and nose.

○ See page 66 for facts about rain.

Literacy Links

Oral Language/Phonological Awareness

○ Discuss snoring. Ask the children if they know anyone who snores. Encourage the children to make snoring sounds. Print "zzzzz" on chart paper. Tell the children that "zzzzz" is often used to describe the sound of snoring. Sing the first verse of the song while a small group of children snore lightly in the background.

Phonological Awareness/Letter Knowledge

❍ Print *pouring*, *snoring*, and *boring* on a sheet of chart paper. Read the words aloud. Help children recognize the rhyming sounds of the words. Look at the letters in each word. *Which letters are the same?*

Curriculum Connections

Art

❍ Provide containers with several colors of dry tempera paint. Encourage the children to use a dry brush to create a design on their paper. When they are finished, have them lay their designs in a cake pan and spray them with a spray bottle filled with water to simulate the effect of rain. Allow the "Rain Designs" to dry.

❍ Invite the children to draw a picture of an indoor activity they do on a rainy day. Collect the pictures to make a class book titled "Things to Do on a Rainy Day."

> ✓ **Special Needs Adaptation:** Provide magazine pictures of activities that can be done indoors. Invite the children to select a picture that represents something they like to do and might choose to do on a rainy day. Use their selections in the class book.

Discovery

❍ Provide spray bottles with adjustable nozzles filled with water. Encourage the children to spray the bottles onto different surfaces to create a variety of sounds. Challenge them to find a surface and a spray that creates a sound that is gentle and soft like a lullaby.

Dramatic Play

❍ Provide sleeping bags, an alarm clock, pajamas, and other props for sleeping. Encourage the children to pretend to be sleeping. Encourage them to snore!

Gross Motor

❍ Invite the children to play Rain Puddle Jump. Cut rain puddles from 12" x 18" sheets of brown construction paper. Arrange the puddles in a path on the floor. Encourage the children to jump over the rain puddles.

> ✓ **Special Needs Adaptation:** Provide beanbags to children with limited mobility. Encourage them to toss the beanbags over or onto the rain puddles.

Book Corner

Math

○ Encourage the children to play Raindrop Stop. Cut 12 raindrops from blue construction paper. Print the numerals 1-6 on the raindrops to make two sets of playing cards. Give two children a die, an empty coffee can, and one set each of the raindrop cards. Have the children lay their raindrops in front of them on the floor. The first player rolls the die and then picks up the raindrop with the numeral that matches the number on the die, and places the raindrop in the can. The next child rolls the die and does the same thing. When a number is rolled a second time, the player simply passes the die to the other player without removing a raindrop. The winner is the child who runs out of raindrops, or stops the rain, first.

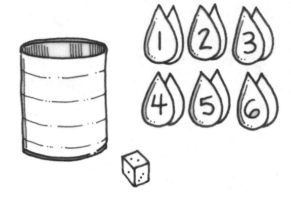

Water Play

○ Provide cups, pitchers, watering cans, plastic bottles, and other utensils for pouring. Have the children describe the speed of the water as it moves through the various spouts. *Does the water pour slowly? Does it pour evenly?* Challenge the children to describe the sound of the water as it hits the water in a container or the bottom of another empty container.

Home Activity

○ Suggest that families collect rainwater to use for watering plants. Suggest that families measure the amount of rain they collect during each rainstorm.

Cap, Mittens, Boots, and Scarf

Vocabulary

boot
cap
coat
fun
mitten
scarf
shoe
sock
sun
warm
winter

Theme Connections

Clothing
Seasons
Winter

by Pam Schiller

(Tune: Head, Shoulders, Knees, and Toes)
Caps, mittens, boots, and scarf,
Boots and scarf!
Caps, mittens, boots, and scarf,
Boots and scarf!
Shoes and socks and coat and sun
Keep me warm for winter fun,
Winter fun!
(Repeat)

Did You Know?

○ Up to 50% of the body's heat production can be lost through an uncovered head. A hat will greatly slow this body heat loss, especially a knit wool cap or a balaclava, a knit cap that covers the head and neck.

○ The hands are often the first part of the body to feel the effects of body heat loss. Mittens will provide more warmth than gloves because the fingers warm each other.

○ Feet are often cold because a person is wearing thin socks and boots that are too tight and restrict circulation. Damp socks, especially cotton socks, will cause feet to be uncomfortable and cold. Wool socks are best in cold, wet weather conditions.

Literacy Links

Oral Language

○ Use the "Cap, Mittens, Boots, and Scarf" rebus cards (pages 112-113) as you sing the song. Point to each picture as the children sing each word. This is especially important for children who are English language learners.

○ Discuss the differences between mittens and gloves. Have a pair of mittens and a pair of gloves for the children to see.

○ Teach the children "Cold Fact" by Dick Emmons. Discuss the length of time it takes to put on all of our winter clothing.

> **Cold Fact** by Dick Emmons
> *By the time he's suited*
> *And scarved and booted*
> *And mittened and capped*
> *And zipped and snapped*
> *And tucked and belted,*
> *The snow has melted.*

○ Make a Word Web (page 118). Print *winter fun* in the center of a sheet of chart paper. Draw a circle around the words. Invite the children to tell you what they know about winter fun. *What kind of things can you do outdoors during the winter?* Draw lines out from the circled words and print the children ideas on the lines.

✔ **Special Needs Adaptation:** For children who are unable to verbalize what they know about winter fun, encourage them to make a picture Word Web. Provide pictures of winter fun activities and pictures of summer fun activities. Ask a child to show you a winter fun picture. When she points to one, put it on the picture Word Web. If she selects a summer fun picture, say, "Yes, it is fun, but we do that in the summer when the weather is warmer."

Curriculum Connections

Art

○ Provide paper and crayons. Encourage the children to draw a winter scene. For an especially cold day picture, provide blue construction paper and white paint.

○ Show the children a pair of decorative socks, and then cut sock shapes from poster board or construction paper. Provide pens, crayons, rickrack, lace, yarn, and other materials. Invite the children to design a pair of decorative socks.

Caps, Hats, Socks, and Mittens by Louise Borden
The Jacket I Wear in the Snow by Shirley Neitzel
The Mitten by Jan Brett
The Season of Arnold's Apple Tree by Gail Gibbons

Dramatic Play
❍ Fill the center with winter clothing for the children to try on. Provide a mirror so the children can view their winter outfits.

Games
❍ Provide a basket of mittens and/or socks. Invite the children to match the mittens and/or socks to make pairs.

Gross Motor
❍ Provide a cap and a box. Use masking tape to create a throw line. Have the children stand at the throw line and toss the cap into the box.

Language
❍ Give the children the "Cap, Mittens, Boots, and Scarf" rebus cards (pages 112-113) and encourage them to sing the song using the pictures. Challenge them to arrange the pictures in the order in which they appear in the song.

Outdoors
❍ Play Drop the Mitten as you would play Drop the Handkerchief. Have the children form a circle. Select one child to be IT. Give IT a mitten. Instruct IT to walk around the circle and drop the mitten behind the child of her choice. The selected child chases IT around the circle and attempts to tag her before she can get back around to that child's place in the circle.

Home Activity

❍ Suggest that the children match mittens, socks, gloves, and shoes at home.

The Seeds Grow

by Pam Schiller

(Tune: The Farmer in the Dell)
The gardener plants the seeds.
The gardener plants the seeds.
Deep down inside the ground
The gardener plants the seeds.

The clouds bring the rain.
The clouds bring the rain.
Thirsty seeds need water to drink
So, the clouds bring the rain.

The sun warms the earth.
The sun warms the earth.
The seeds sleep below the ground
And the sun warms the earth.

The gardener pulls the weeds.
The gardener pulls the weeds.
Little plants need room to grow
So, the gardener pulls the weeds.

The seeds grow into flowers.
The seeds grow into flowers.
Colorful, sweet and oh, so neat—
A garden full of flowers.

Vocabulary

cloud	colorful
drink	flower
garden	gardener
ground	rain
seed	sleep
thirsty	warm
weed	

Theme Connections

Farms
Growing Things
Nature

Did You Know?

- A seed is a budding (young) plant-to-be in a shell.
- Seeds are not only a source for future flowers, vegetables, fruits, and trees, but are also a source of immediate food for animals and people. Some birds thrive on seeds, squirrels and chipmunks eat nuts, and human beings eat pumpkin seeds, sunflower seeds, flax seeds, and a variety of nuts, which are also seeds.
- Seeds and nuts have lots of nutritional value, and are high in protein.

Literacy Links

Oral Language

- Make a Word Web (page 118). Print *seeds* in the center of a sheet of chart paper. Draw a circle around the word. Have the children tell you what they know about seeds. Print their information on lines drawn out from the circle.

○ Teach the children "Do a Good Deed." Suit the actions to the words.

Do a Good Deed
Dig a little hole,
Plant a little seed.
Give it some water.
What a good deed!

 English Language Learner Strategy: Model the actions for the child until he is able to follow along independently.

Print Awareness

○ Show the children seed catalogs. Point out the vast variety of seeds and the many plants and trees that come from seeds.

Curriculum Connections

Art

○ Encourage the children to draw or paint a picture of a flower garden. Provide a variety of colors of crayons or paints.

Construction

○ Help children create a bird feeder. Tie a 24" string around the top of a pinecone. Roll the pinecone first in peanut butter and then in birdseed. Hang the feeder in a tree.

Dramatic Play

○ Provide gardener's clothing, such as hat, gloves, and overalls, and gardener's tools, such as a rake, hand shovel, and a watering can. Encourage the children to pretend to be gardeners. Provide silk or plastic flowers and seeds for inspiration.

Gross Motor

○ Provide a variety of seeds, such as nuts, acorns, and sunflower seeds. Invite the children to hold each seed chest high and attempt to drop it into a jar below. *Which seeds drop straight? Which seeds are heaviest?*

Math

○ Label jars with stick-on numerals from 1-10 to make Counting Jars. Provide seeds, tweezers, and Counting Jars. Encourage the children to use the tweezers to pick up the seeds as they count the appropriate number of seeds into each jar.

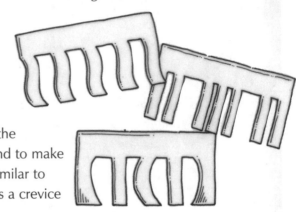

Book Corner

✓ **Special Needs Adaptation:** For children with physical limitations, place seeds on a sheet of construction paper. Provide additional sheets of construction paper with numerals 1-10 written on them to make Counting Mats. Provide a tongue depressor for children to use to move the correct number of seeds from the sheet of construction paper onto each Counting Mat.

Sand Table

❍ Make Sand Combs. Cut several 4" x 8" poster board strips. Cut a comb pattern in one of the 8" sides. Vary the pattern in each comb. Show the children how to comb the sand to make patterns. Explain that this is similar to the way a plow works—it cuts a crevice in the soil for planting seeds.

Science

❍ Display pictures of some animals that eat nuts and others that do not eat nuts. Discuss each animal. *What do animals need to be able to crack the nuts? Can an animal without teeth eat nuts?* Give the children the pictures and have them sort the animals into those that eat nuts and those that do not eat nuts.

❍ Provide potting soil, small containers and marigold seeds. Invite the children to plant the marigold seeds.

✓ **Special Needs Adaptation:** Make picture cards showing each step. Encourage the child to put the cards in sequential order before starting the activity. Give him the cards to help him as he plants his seeds. If he needs extra support, help him with the first step, and then encourage him to do the next step independently.

Snack

❍ Provide edible seeds, such as pumpkin, flax, sunflower, and sesame, for snack. **Allergy warning**: Check for allergies before serving.

Home Activity

❍ Suggest that families plant seeds and ask their children to help care for the seeds as they grow into flowers or vegetables.

Cuckoo Round

Vocabulary

cuckoo	evening
forest	low
moon	soon
summer	sun

Theme Connections

Nighttime
Seasons
Summer

Upon a summer's evening I walked the forest through,
When suddenly I heard a sweet and low cuckoo.

Cuckoo, cuckoo, cuckoo, cuckoo, cuckoo,
Cuckoo, cuckoo, cuckoo, cuckoo, cuckoo.

Mr. Moon, you're out too soon; the sun is still in the sky!
Go back to bed and cover your head and wait 'til the stars go by.

Cuckoo, cuckoo, cuckoo, cuckoo, cuckoo,
Cuckoo, cuckoo, cuckoo, cuckoo, cuckoo.
(Repeat)

Did You Know?

○ The name *cuckoo* is used for many of the 127 species of birds of the cuckoo family (Cuculidae, order Cuculiformes). Some cuckoos are brood parasites—birds that build no nests of their own but leave their eggs in the nests of other birds, which then rear the young. Nest parasitism is characteristic of less than half of all cuckoo species. Some cuckoos are arboreal, which means that they live in trees; but others, such as the roadrunner of the Southwestern United States, are poor fliers.

○ Arboreal cuckoos eat insects. The larger species, such as the roadrunner, live on the ground and feed on snakes, lizards, small rodents, and other birds, which they bludgeon with their strong bills.

○ Most cuckoos are drab gray or brown and have long tails and downward curved bills. The glossy cuckoos, however, are a striking emerald green.

○ True to the stereotype, the cuckoo's nest is slovenly, arranged with twigs and sometimes a few green leaves, usually added around the time babies are hatching. The nest is scarcely adequate. Nests are sometimes placed in a clump of deciduous bushes or on a low branch of an apple tree in an orchard, rarely in an evergreen, and always at low elevations.

Literacy Links

Letter Knowledge
O Print *cuckoo* on chart paper. *Which letters appear in the word more than one time? Which letters appear only once?*

Oral Language
O Talk about the cuckoo. Show a photo of the cuckoo bird. Discuss the bird's colors, diet, and habits. Tell the children that the cuckoo bird is so lazy that it often tries to dump its eggs in another bird's nest to avoid building a nest and caring for a baby. Many times, other birds find an odd bird in their nest and feed and care for it, even though it is not theirs.
O Tell the children that the cuckoo is the bird that is often found in clocks—cuckoo clocks. Share the poem, "The Cuckoo Bird," with the children.

> **The Cuckoo Bird**
> *The cuckoo is a funny bird, she sings as she flies.*
> *She'll bring you glad tidings, she'll tell you no lies.*
> *She sips from the pretty flowers to make her voice clear,*
> *And she'll never sing "cuckoo" till the spring of the year.*

Phonological Awareness
O Print *moon* and *soon* on chart paper. Explain that *moon* and *soon* are rhyming words. Have the children think of other words that rhyme with *moon* and *soon*.

Curriculum Connections

Discovery
O Provide a cuckoo clock for the children to examine. Wind it so it will run and announce the time on the hour.

Dramatic Play
O Decorate a large box to look like a cuckoo clock. Cut a door in the box and encourage the children to pretend they are cuckoo birds that pop out each hour to announce the hour by saying "cuckoo." Explain that the number of cuckoos indicate the hour. Have the children outside the box tell the child pretending to be the cuckoo what time it is before he comes out of the box. Have the child pretending to be the cuckoo say "cuckoo" the appropriate number of times.

Book Corner

Cuckoo/Cucú by Lois Ehlert
The Cuckoo Bird by Judy Corbalis
Mr. Cuckoo by Becky Bloom
Sam Pig and the Cuckoo Clock by Alison Uttley

Fine Motor
○ Provide pecans and a nutcracker. Discuss the strong jaws of the cuckoo bird and how he uses his beak as a tool for breaking through tough surfaces. Explain that the bird's beak is similar to a nutcracker. Invite the children to crack the pecans using the nutcracker.

Games
○ Place four plastic eggs in a basket. Place red beads inside three of the eggs and a brown or yellow bead inside the fourth egg. Encourage the children to try to guess which egg has the odd bird inside. After the correct egg is identified, encourage the children to place the beads inside the eggs again and again try to guess which egg has the odd bird inside.

Gross Motor
○ Use masking tape to create a zigzag line on the floor. Provide plastic eggs. Challenge the children to roll the egg down the zigzag line by nudging it with their toe a few inches at a time.

Listening
○ Provide a recorder and encourage children to tape themselves saying "cuckoo, cuckoo." Encourage them to use a variety of different types of voices, for example, high, sing-song, low, whispering, and so on.

Math
○ Place playdough balls of different sizes inside six plastic eggs. Challenge the children to arrange the eggs from the lightest to heaviest.

Music and Movement
○ Talk with the children about how cuckoo birds move. Explain that many of the birds do not fly, but move like chickens and stay on low branches of trees or on the ground. Cuckoo birds sometimes run like a roadrunner and hop like a bunny. Play music and have the children move like cuckoo birds.

Writing
○ Print *cuckoo* on index cards. Provide tracing paper, tempera paint, and feathers to use as quills. Invite the children to trace over the letters of *cuckoo* with their quills.

Home Activity

○ Encourage the children to look for a cuckoo clock at home. *Does anyone have one?* Ask children to ask their family members if there was a cuckoo clock in their home when they were growing up.

Swinging Along

Swing along the open road under sky that's clear.
Swing along the open road in the fall of the year.
Swing along, swing along, swing along the open road,
All in the fall of the year.

Swinging along the open road, swinging along under sky that's clear,
Swinging along the open road, all in the fall, in the fall of the year,
Swinging along, swinging along the open road
All in the fall of the year.

Vocabulary

clear
fall
open road
sky
swinging along
year

Theme Connections

Fall
Nature
Seasons

Did You Know?

○ "Swinging along" refers to hiking.
○ This is a popular camp song that is often sung while hiking.

Literacy Links

Oral Language

○ Discuss the phrases "swinging along" and "open road." Explain that this is a great song to sing while you are hiking or taking a nature walk.
○ Discuss the things a person might see on the open road in the fall of the year. *How would these things change if the song said "in the spring of the year?"*
○ Teach the children the song, "I'm Happy When I'm Hiking" (page 102). Discuss hiking. *Why do people enjoy hiking? Where do people like to hike? Have you ever gone hiking?*

Print Awareness/Oral Language

○ Teach the children the hiking cadence "Sound Off" (page 104). Encourage them to work as a group to create new verses for the cadence. Print their verses on chart paper. Point to the words as the children chant the new verses.

Curriculum Connections

Art
❍ Provide blue and white tempera paint, brushes, and paper. Encourage the children to paint a picture of a clear blue sky.

Dramatic Play
❍ Set up a camp area with props, such as a tent, backpacks, sleeping bags, cooking equipment, and other camping-related items. Invite the children to pretend that they are camping out under the stars.

Language
❍ Make a rebus list of things one might pack in a backpack. Provide a backpack, the rebus packing list (page 110), and the items on the list. Encourage the children to pack their backpacks. Make sure to put out some items that are not on the list and use numerals in your list, for example, two water bottles, three small towels, and so on.

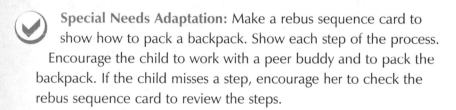

Special Needs Adaptation: Make a rebus sequence card to show how to pack a backpack. Show each step of the process. Encourage the child to work with a peer buddy and to pack the backpack. If the child misses a step, encourage her to check the rebus sequence card to review the steps.

Listening
❍ Provide camping and hiking songs for the children to listen to. You may want to use the *Bountiful Earth* CD, which is in the back of this book.

Science
❍ Go on a nature walk. Discuss the wonders of nature as you walk along. Sing "Swinging Along" and other hiking songs.

Snack
❍ Invite the children to make trail mix. Give each child a resealable plastic bag. Have them pour into their bags two tablespoons of wheat cereal, rice cereal, mini-pretzels, raisins, and peanuts. **Allergy warning:** Be sure

Book Corner

Amelia Bedelia Goes Camping by Peggy Parrish
Johnny Appleseed by Steven Kellogg
Sally Goes to the Mountains by Stephen Huneck

to check for allergies. Make a more creative mix by adding dried banana chips, dried apples or apricots, chocolate or butterscotch chips, and/or marshmallows.

 English Language Learner Strategy: Provide a rebus of how to make the trail mix so the child can follow the directions independently.

Social Studies

❍ Provide travel brochures. Ask the children to choose a place they would like to travel to.

Home Connection

❍ Suggest that families talk with their children about hiking trips they have experienced. Suggest that the family plan a hiking trip.

America the Beautiful

Vocabulary

amber
brotherhood
crown
fruited
spacious
grace
plain
sea
shed
shining
thy
waves of grain

Theme Connections

Growing Things
Nature
Patriotism

O beautiful for spacious skies,
For amber waves of grain,
For purple mountain majesties
Above the fruited plain!
America! America!
God shed his grace on thee,
And crown thy good with brotherhood
From sea to shining sea!

Did You Know?

○ "America the Beautiful" was written by the professor, poet, and writer, Katharine Lee Bates. Bates wrote the song in 1893 while on a trip to Colorado Springs, Colorado. When she got to the top of Pike's Peak, she said, "All the wonder of America seemed displayed there, with the sea-like expanse." The view was so beautiful it inspired her to write the song that is considered by some to be the United States' unofficial national anthem.

○ For two years after "America the Beautiful" was written, it was sung to any popular or folk tune that fit with the lyrics. "Auld Lang Syne" was the most popular of these tunes. In 1926, the National Federation of Music Clubs held a contest to put the poem to music. None of the entries seemed to fit the poem. Today, "America the Beautiful" is sung to Samuel A. Ward's hymn, "Materna."

○ America, the New World, was named by cartographer, Martin Waldseemueller, in 1507.

Literacy Links

Oral Language

○ Discuss things that are considered trademarks of America; for example, apple pie, baseball, hot dogs, barbeque, and the American flag.

✔ **English Language Learner Strategy:** Provide pictures of what you are talking about so it will be easier for the child to understand the meaning of the words.

○ Discuss *patriotism*. Tell the children that patriotism is love of and dedication to one's country. Teach the children other patriotic songs (page 102). Discuss the words in the songs that may be new vocabulary for the children.

○ Show the children a map of the United States. Point out the state in which they live.

✔ **Special Needs Adaptation:** Use a large map. Encourage the child to use his fingers to trace an outline of the state in which he lives. Puzzles of the United States with the state removed provide good prompts in helping the child understand where his state is located on the map.

Curriculum Connections

Art
○ Provide red and white tempera paint and easel paper. Invite the children to paint red and white stripes to look like the flag.

Fine Motor
○ Provide a commercial puzzle of the United States. Discuss the states. Point out the state in which you live.

Library
○ Provide books that have pictures of the countryside of the United States.

Math
○ Provide 50 paper stars. Lay 10 of the stars in a line. Have the children lay four more rows of ten stars under the one you laid. Point out that these stars represent the 50 states that make up the United States. If an American flag is available, point out the stars on the flag.

Music and Movement
○ Play patriotic music and encourage the children to dance with red, white, and blue streamers.

Snack
○ Make apple turnovers. Give each child a refrigerated biscuit. Show them how to use their hands to flatten the biscuit. Have them spoon two tablespoons of apple pie filling onto one half of the biscuit. Show them how to fold the biscuit in half and pinch the edges to seal in the filling. Have an adult place the pies in a deep fryer for six minutes (adult only). Turn the pies once while they are frying. Remove from the fryer and drain. Cool and eat. **Safety note**: Supervise closely.

Writing
○ Print *America* on a sheet of chart paper. Provide magnetic letters and encourage the children to copy the word with the letters.

Home Activity

○ Have the children interview their families about living in America. What are their favorite things about America? Which patriotic songs do they like best? When did each child's family come to America?

More Learning and Fun

Songs

America

My county 'tis of thee,
Sweet land of liberty,
Of thee I sing.
Land where by fathers died!
Land of the pilgrims' pride!
From every mountainside
Let freedom ring!

The Ash Grove

Down yonder green valley where streamlets
    meander,
When twilight is fading, I pensively rove.
Or at the bright noontide in solitude wander
Amid the dark shades of the lovely Ash grove.
'Tis there while the blackbird is joyfully singing,
Each warble enchants with his note from the tree
Oh then little think I of sorrow or sadness
The ash grove enchanting spells beauty to me.

Green Trees

Green trees around us,
Blue skies above,
Friends all around us,
In a world filled with love.
Birds singing sweetly,
Hearts ringing true,
Winds blowing gently
Good day to you.

The Hiking Song
Tune: The Caissons Go Rolling Along

Over hill, over dale
We will hit the open trail
As the children go hiking along.
In and out, up and down

You will never see us frown
As the children go hiking along.

And it's hi, hi, ho
As down the trail we go.
Shout out your name
And shout it strong *(each child shouts his or
    her name)*.
Where 'ere we go,
You will always know,
'Cause you'll hear us sing this song.

I'm Happy When I'm Hiking

Tramp, tramp, tramp, tramp, tramp, tramp,
    tramp, tramp.
I'm happy when I'm hiking, pack upon my back.
I'm happy when I'm hiking, off the beaten track.
Out in the open country, that's the place for me
With a loyal friend to the journey's end,
Ten, twenty, thirty, forty, fifty miles a day.
Tramp, tramp, tramp...

The More We Get Together

The more we get together, together, together.
The more we get together, the happier we'll be.
For your friends are my friends
And my friends are your friends.
The more we get together, the happier we'll be.

Pearly Shell

Pearly shell by the ocean
Shining in the sunlight covering the shore.
When I see you my heart tells me
I love you more than all the other pearly shells.

The Robin

There came to my window
One morning in spring
A sweet little robin,
She came here to sing.
The tune that she sang
It was prettier far,
Than any I've heard
On the flute or guitar.

Her wings she was spreading
To soar far away,
Then resting a moment
Seemed sweetly to say,
"Oh happy, how happy
The world seems to be,
Awake, dearest, child,
And be happy with me."

Sledding

Tune: Row, Row, Row Your Boat
Crunch, crunch, crunch the snow
Up the hill we go.
Sliding, sliding, sliding, sliding
Down the hill of snow.

There's No Place Like Home

'Mid pleasures and palaces
Though we may roam,
Be it ever so humble,
There's no place like home.
A charm from the skies
Seems to hallow us there,
Which seek thro' the world,
Is ne'er met with elsewhere.
Home, home, sweet, sweet home,
There's no place like home,
There's no place like home.

You're a Grand Old Flag

You're a grand old flag,
You're a high flying flag,
And forever in peace may you wave.
You're the emblem of
The land I love,
The home of the free and the brave.
Ev'ry heart beats true
'Neath the red, white, and blue
Where there's never a boast or brag.
But should old acquaintance be forgot,
Keep your eye on the grand old flag.

Poems, Chants, and Rhymes

Birdie, Birdie, Where Is Your Nest?

Birdie, birdie, where is your nest?
Birdie, birdie, where is your nest?
Birdie, birdie, where is your nest?
In the tree that I love best.

Fall by Pam Schiller

Fall is here
Frost is in the air.
Chill is on my cheeks,
Static in my hair.

Colorful leaves fall like rain.
Sun and clouds play hide and seek.
The wind blows across the grass.
Apples are ripe and at their peak.

I help at home to rake the leaves.
We put them in a sack.
We sweep the roof and clean the eaves.
Before we finish…the leaves are back.

Fall is in the air,
Static in my hair.
Leaves on the lawn,
And autumn frost at dawn.

Hiking Chant—Sound Off

Chorus:
Sound off (leader)
1 — 2 (by group)
Sound off (leader)
3 — 4 (by group)
Cadence count (leader)
1 — 2 — 3 — 4, 1 — 2 —- 3 — 4 (everyone)

Boys and girls they love to play.
They turn cartwheels every day.

Chorus

I'm so hungry—I want lunch
Give me something good to crunch.

Chorus

(Continue to make up verses.)

I'm a Frozen Icicle

I'm a frozen icicle
Hanging by your door.
When it's cold, I grow some more.
When it's warm, I'm on the floor!

Jack Frost

Jack Frost bites your noses.
He chills your cheeks and freezes your toes.
He comes every year when winter is here
And stays until spring is near.

Nature Walk

Going for a walk is so much fun.
We don't hurry and we don't run.
We look at all the pretty trees
And listen for birds and buzzing bees.

The North Wind Doth Blow

The north wind doth blow,
And we shall have snow.
And what will the robin do then, poor thing?
He will sit in the barn and keep himself warm,
With his little head tucked under his wing,
    poor thing!

Whether the Weather

Whether the weather be fine,
Or whether the weather be not.
Whether the weather be cold,
Or whether the weather be hot.
We'll weather the weather,
Whatever the weather,
Whether we like it or not.

Fingerplays and Action Rhymes

Autumn Leaves

Autumn leaves are falling, falling, falling. (move
    from standing to squatting)
Autumn leaves are spinning, spinning, spinning.
    (stand and turn)
Autumn leaves are floating, floating, floating.
    (sway side to side)
Autumn leaves are turning, turning, turning. (turn
    slowly)
Autumn leaves are dancing, dancing, dancing.
    (stand on toes, sway forward and back)
Autumn leaves are blowing, blowing, blowing.
    (take several steps forward)
Autumn leaves are falling, falling, falling. (squat)
Autumn leaves are sleeping, sleeping, sleeping.
    (place hands together on side of head)

Cloud

What's fluffy white and floats up high *(point skyward)*
Like a pile of cotton in the sky?
And when the wind blows hard and strong, *(wiggle fingers moving horizontally)*
What very gently floats along? *(wiggle fingers moving downward)*
What brings the rain? *(open hands palm up)*
What brings the snow
That showers down on us below?
When you look up in the high blue sky, *(look up)*
What is that thing you see float by? *(answer)*
A cloud.

Five Little Snowmen

(Hold up five fingers and move one for each snowman. At the end, hold out your hands like saying "all gone!")
Five little snowmen happy and gay,
The first one said, "What a nice day!"
The second one said, "We'll cry no tears,"
The third one said, "We'll stay for years."
The fourth one said, "But what happens in May?"
The fifth one said, "Look, we're melting away!"

Five Waiting Pumpkins

(Suit actions to the words.)
Five little pumpkins growing on a vine,
First one said, "It's time to shine!"
Second one said, "I love the fall"
Third one said, "I'm round as a ball."
Fourth one said, "I want to be a pie."
Fifth one said, "Let's say good-bye."
"Good-bye," said one!
"Adios," said two!
"Au revoir," said three!
"Ciao," said four!
"Aloha," said five!
And five little pumpkins were picked that day!

Listening Stories

Johnny Appleseed
adapted by Pam Schiller

Johnny Appleseed lived almost 150 years ago. Even though he lived so long ago, the fruit of his work, the apple tree, is still with us today. He is famous for planting apple trees all over the country!

Johnny Appleseed's real name is John Chapman. People called him Johnny Appleseed because he loved apple trees.

Johnny was a simple man who spent most of his time alone under the stars and trees he loved so much. He was a friend to everyone he met and to every creature he encountered. People say that animals would walk right up to Johnny. They were not afraid of him at all.

Fun things to know about Johnny Appleseed.
- Johnny wore a cooking pot on his head in place of a hat. Can you imagine that? The truth is, he probably tied it to his back for most of his journey.
- He was a small man and people often show pictures of him in clothing that looks two sizes too big.
- Johnny Appleseed preferred to walk rather than ride. He walked along planting apple seeds everywhere he went. Some people say we would not have the abundance of apples we have today if it hadn't been for the work he did 150 years ago.

Johnny loved all people, but the people he loved best were children. He would tell them stories and read to them by firelight at night after dinner.

Next time you take a bite of an apple, you might want to say a quiet thank you to Johnny Appleseed.

The Wind and the Sun

The Wind and the Sun were arguing about which one of them was stronger. Suddenly, they saw a traveler coming down the road, and the Sun said, "I see a way to decide our dispute. Whichever of us can cause that traveler to take off his coat shall be regarded as the stronger. You begin." So the Sun retired behind a cloud, and the Wind began to blow as hard as it could upon the traveler. But the harder he blew, the more closely the traveler wrapped his coat around him. At last the Wind had to give up in despair. Then the Sun came out and shone in all his glory upon the traveler, who soon found it too hot to walk with his coat on.

Facts Related to Bountiful Earth

Apples

- ○ Two pounds of apples make one 9" pie.
- ○ The apple blossom is the state flower of Michigan.
- ○ 2,500 varieties of apples are grown in the United States.
- ○ 7,500 varieties of apples are grown throughout the world.
- ○ 100 varieties of apples are grown commercially in 36 of the United States.
- ○ Apples are fat-, sodium-, and cholesterol-free.
- ○ Apples are a great source of the fiber pectin. One apple has five grams of fiber.

Seeds

- ○ Seeds that are not planted by humans can still find a way to start new plants. Here are some of the ways that seeds disperse:
  - ○ **Hitchhikers** stick to fur, feathers, or clothing and fall off later at a new place.
  - ○ **Droppers** simply fall to the ground; however, animals usually carry these dropped seeds to other places.
  - ○ **Poppers** burst from their seed container and travel away from the plant.
  - ○ **Flyers** are carried in the wind by their wings or their feathery parachutes.

Stars

- ○ No one knows how many stars are in the sky. It is like counting the grains of sand on the beach. Some scientists estimate that there are more than 400 billion stars in the Milky Way.
- ○ Stars vary in color according to their surface temperature. The hottest stars are blue-white, followed by white, yellow-white, orange, and then red. The sun is a star. The reason most stars appear white to us is because we have two kinds of light sensors in our eyes. Sensors called "rods" detect brightness, while sensors called "cones" detect color. The cones are not very sensitive, so if a light is too dim they are not activated, and we perceive the color as white. So, even a red star looks white if it is dim, and only brighter stars look to us like they have color!

Sequence Cards
Seed-to-Fruit

Rhyming Word Game

Down by the Bay

Rhyming Word Game
Down by the Bay

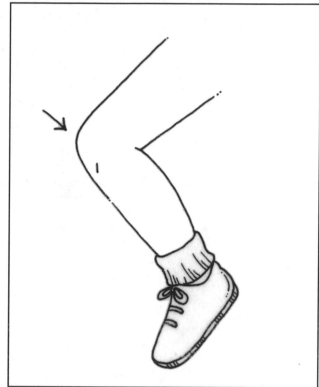

Backpack Packing List Rebus

(Using a rebus makes it easier for English language learners to follow directions.)

Backpack Packing List

Baggie Ice Cream Rebus

(Using a rebus makes it easier for English language learners to follow directions.)

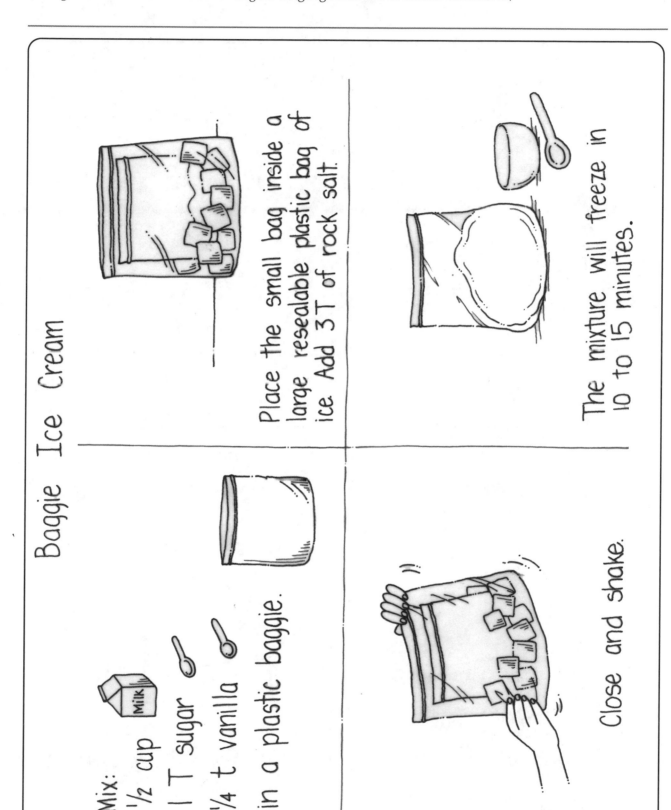

Baggie Ice Cream

Mix:
½ cup 🥛
1 T sugar 🥄
¼ t vanilla 🥄
in a plastic baggie.

Place the small bag inside a large resealable plastic bag of ice. Add 3 T of rock salt.

Close and shake.

The mixture will freeze in 10 to 15 minutes.

Cap, Mittens, Boots, and Scarf Rebus

(Using a rebus makes it easier for English language learners to follow directions.)

Hat

Mittens

Boots

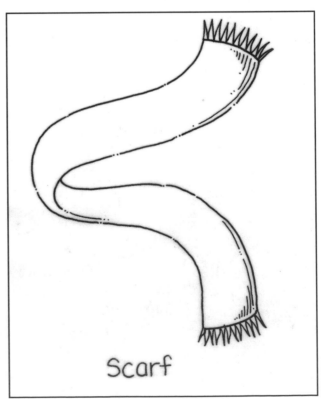

Scarf

Cap, Mittens, Boots, and Scarf Rebus

(Using a rebus makes it easier for English language learners to follow directions.)

shoes

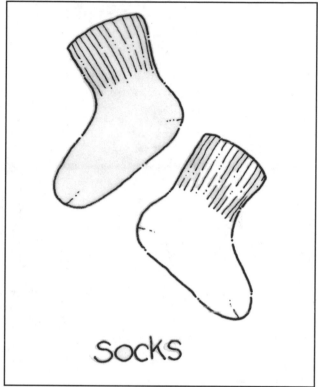

Socks

Coat

Sun

Cloud Dough Rebus

(Using a rebus makes it easier for English language learners to follow directions.)

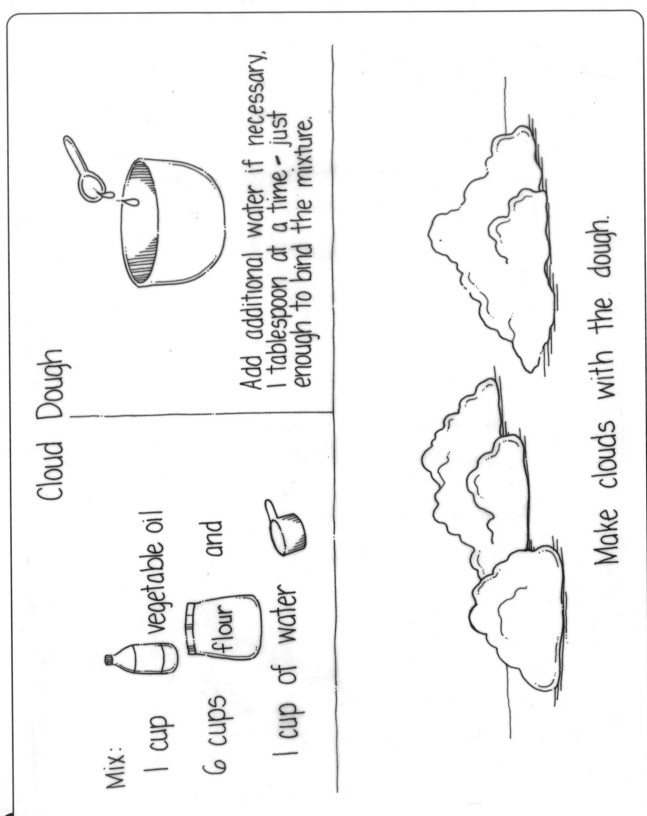

Cloud Dough

Mix:

1 cup vegetable oil

6 cups flour and

1 cup of water

Add additional water if necessary, 1 tablespoon at a time – just enough to bind the mixture.

Make clouds with the dough.

Pumpkin Milkshake Rebus

(Using a rebus makes it easier for English language learners to follow directions.)

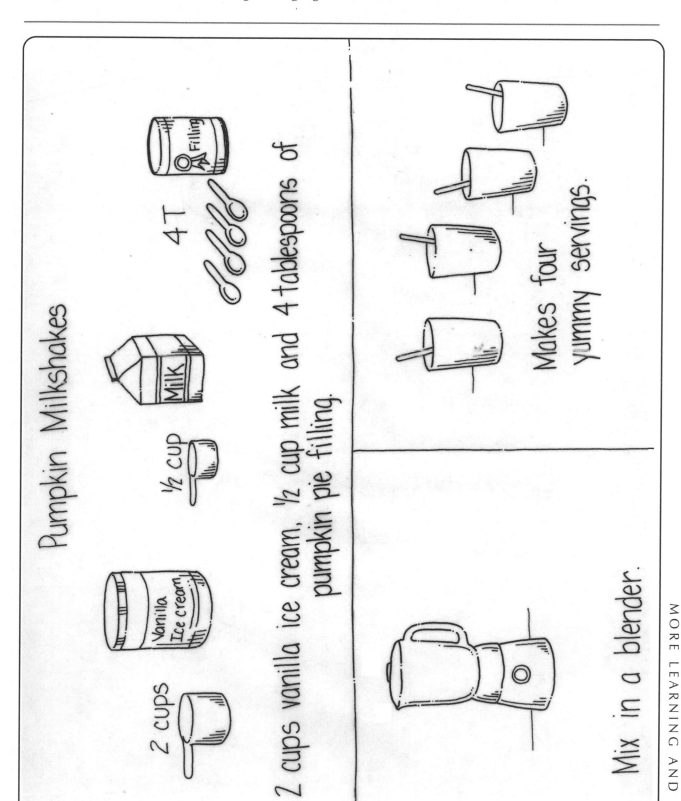

Pumpkin Milkshakes

2 cups vanilla ice cream, ½ cup milk and 4 tablespoons of pumpkin pie filling.

Mix in a blender.

Makes four yummy servings.

Snow Dough Rebus

(Using a rebus makes it easier for English language learners to follow directions.)

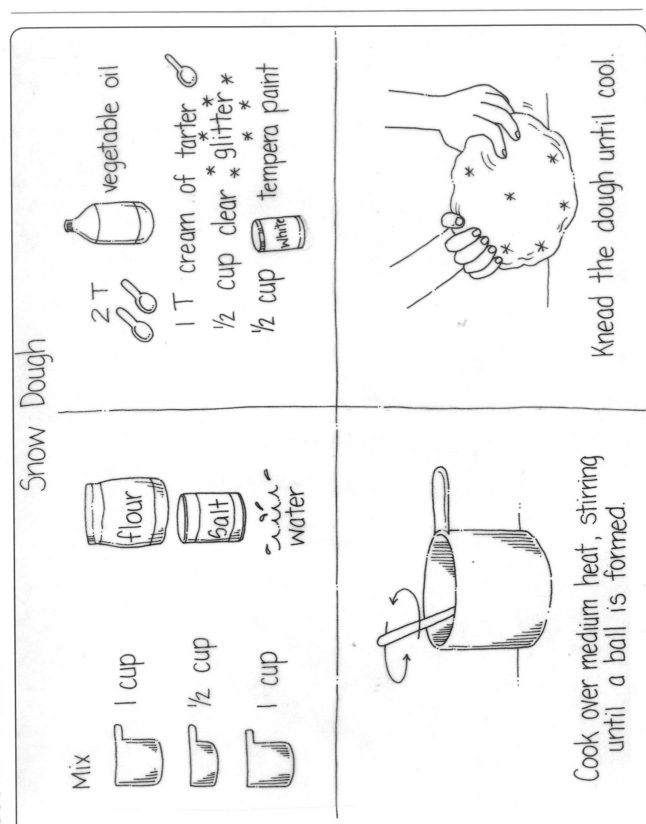

Snow Dough

vegetable oil

2 T

1 T cream of tarter

½ cup clear * glitter *

½ cup white tempera paint

flour

salt

water

Mix

1 cup

½ cup

1 cup

Knead the dough until cool.

Cook over medium heat, stirring until a ball is formed.

The Weather Song Rebus

(Using a rebus makes it easier for English language learners to follow directions.)

Sunny

Rainy

Snowy

Foggy

Word Web Pattern

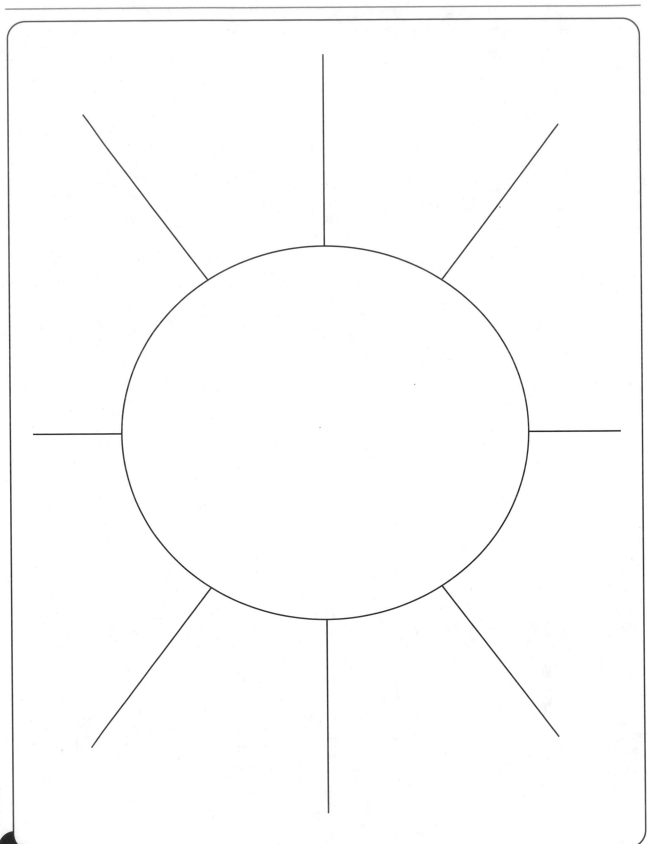

KWL Chart Pattern

KWL Chart

What We Know	What We Want to Know	What We Learned

American Sign Language Signs

flower

earth
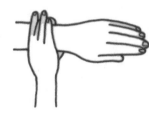

sandwich

lollipop

moon

love

I

hill

American Sign Language Signs

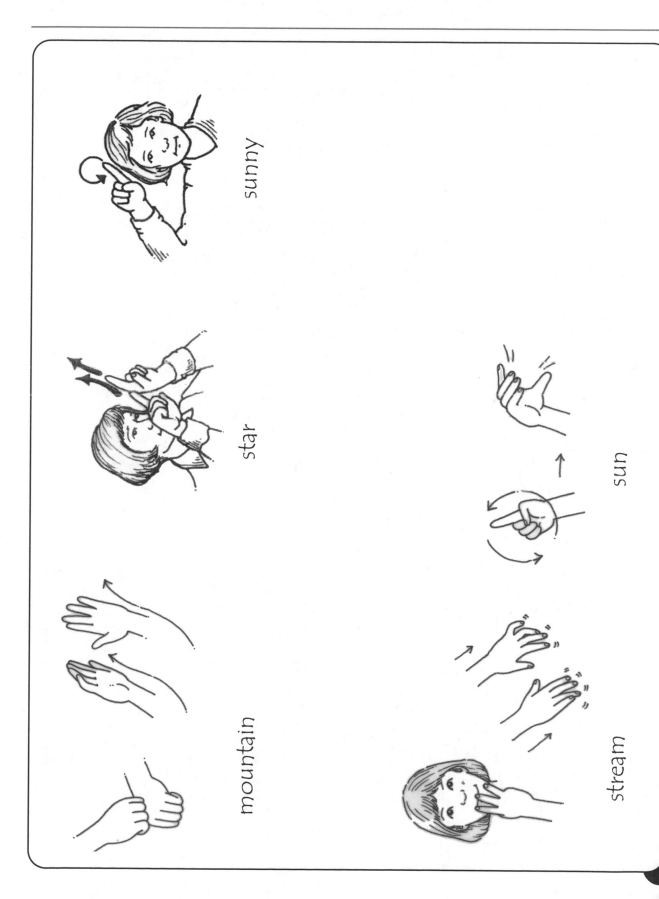

sunny

star

sun

mountain

stream

Alphabet Finger Signs

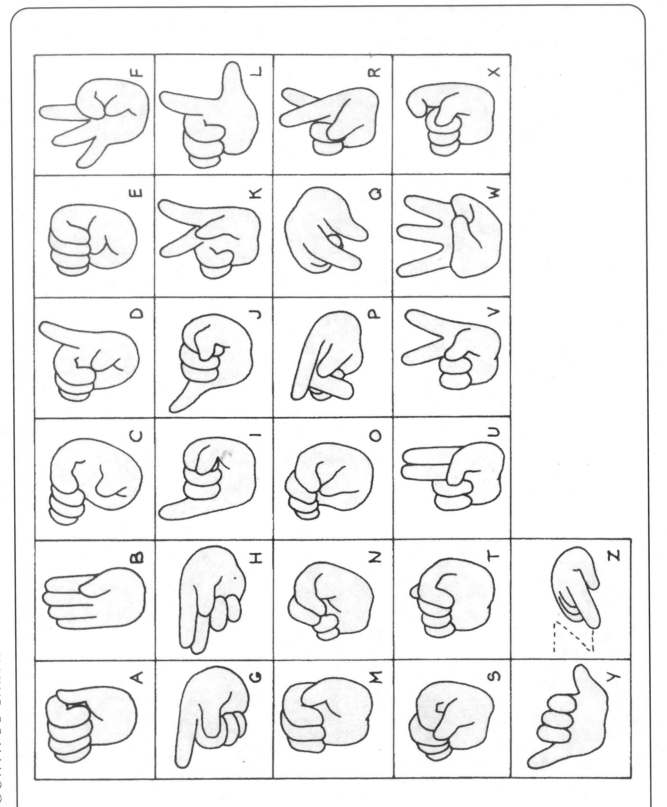

References and Bibliography

Bulloch, Kathleen. (2003) *The Mystery of Modifying: Creative Solutions.* Education Service Center, Region VI: Huntsville, Texas.

Cavallaro, Claire and Haney, Michael. (1999) *Preschool Inclusion.* Paul H. Brookes Publishing Co: Baltimore, MD.

Gray, Tracy and Fleischman, Steve. "Research Matters; Successful Strategies for English Language Learners." *Educational Leadership,* Dec. 2004-Jan. 2005, Volume 62, 84-85.

Hanniford, Carla. (1995). *Smart moves: Why learning is not all in your head.* Great Ocean Publications: Arlington, Virginia, p. 146.

Keller, Matthew. (2004). "Warm Weather Boosts Mood, Broadens the Mind." *Post Doctoral Study: The University of Michigan,* Ann Arbor, MI.

LeDoux, Joseph. (1993). "Emotional memory systems in the brain" *Behavioral and Brain Research,* volume 58.

Theme Index

Children's Book Index

Index